Playing with Plays
Presents
Lewis Carroll's

Alice's Adventures in Wonderland

FOR KIDS
(The melodramatic version!)

For 7-21+ actors, or kids of all ages who want to have fun!
Creatively modified by
Angela M. Herrick & Brendan P. Kelso
Cover stage illustrated by Shana Hallmeyer
Cover Characters by Ron Leishman
Lewis Carroll Character by Ryan Gottlieb
Cake illustrated by Keagan P. Kelso

3 Melodramatic Modifications of Shakespeare's Play
for 3 different group sizes:

7-12+ Actors

10-16+ Actors

13-21+ Actors

Table Of Contents

Foreword .... Pg 4

School, Afterschool, and Summer classes .... Pg 6

Performance Rights .... Pg 6

7-12+ Actors .... Pg 8

10-16+ Actors .... Pg 30

13-17+ Actors .... Pg 56

Special Thanks .... Pg 83

Sneak Peeks at other Playing With Plays .... Pg 84

About the Authors .... Pg 103

For Princess Meah -
For reminding me how important it is for girls to see female heroes and villains in their stories. And for teaching me that one can be one's own favorite princess. You inspire me every day.
- AMH

To V,
May your life always be full of the same wonder
your smile
brings to the world.
-BPK

Playing with Plays™ – Lewis Carroll's Alice's Adventures in Wonderland for Kids

Copyright © 2004-2020 by Brendan P. Kelso, Playing with Plays LLC
Some characters on the cover are ©Ron Leishman ToonClipart.com

All rights reserved. No part of this book may be reproduced in any form or by any electronic or mechanical means, including photocopying, recording, information storage or retrieval systems now known or to be invented, without permission in writing from the publisher, except by a reviewer, who may quote brief passages in a review, written for inclusion within a periodical. Any members of education institutions wishing to photocopy part or all of the work for classroom use, or publishers who would like to obtain permission to include the work in an anthology, should send their inquiries to the publisher. We monitor the internet for cases of piracy and copyright infringement/violations. We will pursue all cases within the full extent of the law.

Whenever a Playing With Plays play is produced, the following must be included on all programs, printing and advertising for the play: © Brendan P. Kelso, Playing with Plays LLC, www.PlayingWithPlays.com. All rights reserved.

CAUTION: Professionals and amateurs are hereby warned that these plays are subject to a royalty. They are fully protected, in whole, in part, or in any form under the copyright laws of the United States, Canada, the British Empire, and all other countries of the Copyright Union, and are subject to royalty. All rights, including professional, amateur, motion picture, radio, television, recitation, public reading, internet, and any method of photographic reproduction are strictly reserved.

For performance rights please see page 6 of this book or contact:

contact@PlayingWithPlays.com

-Please note, for certain circumstances, we do waive copyright and performance fees.
Rules subject to change

www.PlayingWithPlays.com

Printed in the United States of America
Published by Playing With Plays LLC

ISBN: 9781688746565

Foreword

When I was in high school there was something about Shakespeare that appealed to me. Not that I understood it mind you, but there were clear scenes and images that always stood out in my mind. Romeo & Juliet, "Romeo, Romeo; wherefore art thou Romeo?"; Julius Caesar, "Et tu Brute"; Macbeth, "Double, Double, toil and trouble"; Hamlet, "to be or not to be"; A Midsummer Night's Dream, all I remember about this was a wickedly cool fairy and something about a guy turning into a donkey that I thought was pretty funny. It was not until I started analyzing Shakespeare's plays as an actor that I realized one very important thing, I still didn't understand them. Seriously though, it's tough enough for adults, let alone kids. Then it hit me, why don't I make a version that kids could perform, but make it easy for them to understand with a splash of Shakespeare lingo mixed in? And voila! A melodramatic masterpiece was created! They are intended to be melodramatically fun!

THE PLAYS: There are 3 plays within this book, for three different group sizes. The reason: to allow educators or parents to get the story across to their children regardless of the size of their group. As you read through the plays, there are several lines that are highlighted. These are actual lines from the original book. I am a little more particular about the kids saying these lines verbatim. But the rest, well... have fun!

The entire purpose of this book is to instill the love of a classic story, as well as drama, into the kids.

And when you have children who have a passion for something, they will start to teach themselves, with or without school.

These plays are intended for pure fun. Please DO NOT have the kids learn these lines verbatim, that would be a complete waste of creativity. But do have them basically know their lines and improvise wherever they want as long as it pertains to telling the story. Because that is the goal of an actor: to tell the story. In A Midsummer Night's Dream, I once had a student playing Quince question me about one of her lines, "but in the actual story, didn't the Mechanicals state that 'they would hang us'?" I thought for a second and realized that she had read the story with her mom, and she was right. So I let her add the line she wanted and it added that much more fun, it made the play theirs. I have had kids throw water on the audience, run around the audience, sit in the audience, lose their pumpkin pants (size 30 around a size 15 doesn't work very well, but makes for some great humor!) and most importantly, die all over the stage. The kids love it.

One last note: if you want some educational resources, loved our plays, want to tell the world how much your kids loved performing Shakespeare, want to insult someone with our Shakespeare Insult Generator, or are just a fan of Shakespeare, then hop on our website and have fun:

PlayingWithPlays.com

With these notes, I'll see you on the stage, have fun, and break a leg!

SCHOOL, AFTERSCHOOL, and SUMMER classes

I've been teaching these plays as afterschool and summer programs for quite some time. Many people have asked what the program is, therefore, I have put together a basic formula so any teacher or parent can follow and have melodramatic success! As well, many teachers use my books in a variety of ways. You can view the formula and many more resources on my website at: PlayingWithPlays.com

- Brendan

OTHER PLAYS AND FULL LENGTH SCRIPTS

We have over 25 different titles, as well as a full-length play in 4-acts for theatre groups: Shakespeare's Hilarious Tragedies. You can see all of our other titles on our website here: PlayingWithPlays.com/books

As well, you can see a sneak peek at some of those titles at the back of this book.

And, if you ever have any questions, please don't hesitate to ask at: Contact@PlayingWithPlays.com

ROYALTIES

If you have any questions about royalties or performance licenses, here are the basic guidelines:

1) Please contact us! We always LOVE to hear about a school or group performing our books! We would also love to share photos and brag about your program as well! (with your permission, of course)

2) If you are a group and DO NOT charge your kids to be in this production, contact us about discounted copyright fees (one way or another, we will make this work for you!) You are NOT required to buy a book per kid (but, we will still send you some really cool Shakespeare tattoos for your kids!)

3) If you are a group and DO charge your kids to be in the production, (i.e. afterschool program, summer camp) we ask that you purchase a book per kid. Contact us as we will give you a bulk discount (10 books or more) and send some really cool press on Shakespeare tattoos!

4) If you are a group and DO NOT charge the audience to see the plays, please see our website FAQs to see if you are eligible to waive the performance royalties (most performances are eligible).

5) If you are a group and DO charge the audience to see the performance, please see our website FAQs for performance licensing fees (this includes performances for donations and competitions).

Any other questions or comments, please see our website or email us at:

contact@PlayingWithPlays.com

The 15-Minute or so Alice's Adventures in Wonderland

By Lewis Carroll
Creatively modified by
Angela M. Herrick & Brendan P. Kelso

7 - 12 Actors

CAST OF CHARACTERS:

ALICE: a seriously confused little girl
WHITE RABBIT: he's always late!
[1]**DOOR:** a Door, yes, a talking door!
[2]**MOUSE:** a mouse with a sad tale or is it tail?
[3]**DODO:** a wise bird
[4]**BLUE CATERPILLAR:** a rude but helpful caterpillar
[5]**CHESHIRE CAT:** a grinning and vanishing cat
[4]**MAD HATTER:** mad maker of hats, likes tea
[5]**MARCH HARE:** friends with Hatter; also mad
[3]**QUEEN OF HEARTS:** our wicked villain
[2]**KNAVE OF HEARTS:** works for the Queen
[1]**CARD SOLDIER:** works for the Queen, very busy!

The same actors can play the following parts:
[1]DOOR and CARD SOLDIER
[2]MOUSE and KNAVE
[3]DODO and QUEEN
[4]BLUE CATERPILLAR and MAD HATTER
[5]CHESHIRE CAT and MARCH HARE (a very nimble actor will be needed for this exchange!)

ACT 1 SCENE 1

(enter ALICE with book)

ALICE: I don't want to read my History lesson. It's soooo boring! What's the use of a book without pictures or conversations or tales of far off adventures?! I just wish I was big so I wouldn't have to do this stuff anymore! *(sits and reads)* William the Conqueror, whose cause was favoured by the pope...

(ALICE dozes; enter WHITE RABBIT and ALICE wakes)

WHITE RABBIT: I'm late! I'm late! *(looks at watch)* Oh no! So LATE!!!

ALICE: Wow! A talking rabbit! Now, THAT'S something you don't see every day! *(WHITE RABBIT runs around and ALICE chases him; RABBIT exits)* He went down that deep, dark hole. I'm going in! What could possibly go wrong?! *(to audience)* This could be a HARE-raising adventure. Come on! *(exits)* AHHH!!!

ALICE: *(offstage)* I'mmmm stillllllll faaaaaaaliiiiiiiiing! AHHH!!!

ACT 1 SCENE 2

(ALICE and DOOR enter)

DOOR: Open me! Open me!

ALICE: Who said that?

DOOR: Down here!

ALICE: A talking door!?

DOOR: Yep! You are going to find A LOT of strange things in the next 15 minutes! Get used to it!!

(ALICE tries to open DOOR)

ALICE: You're locked. Knock-knock.

DOOR: Seriously? A knock-knock joke? Because I'm a door, right? Hilarious.

ALICE: I thought you'd be OPEN to a good joke. Let me in!!

DOOR: Fine! My key's on the table.

(ALICE gets key, "opens" DOOR, and looks)

ALICE: It's the loveliest garden ever! Oh, no! I'm too big to get through. *(returns to table; sets key down)* Hmmm, there's a bottle that says "Drink Me."

DOOR: Definitely do that!

ALICE: What if it's poison?

DOOR: You're the main character and the play just started. Probably not poison.

ALICE: Good point! OK, bottoms up! *(drinks and gets down on knees)* Hey! I shrank to the right size! *(tries to open the door)* You've locked again?!

DOOR: Where's my key?... Whoops, you left it on the table!

ALICE: Ah, man.

DOOR: Hey, look there's some cake with a note.

ALICE: Oh, I like cake! *(picks it up)* It says, "Eat me."

DOOR: Maybe it'll help you grow. If it doesn't, you still get to eat cake!

ALICE: Good point, Door! *(to audience)* Wait. I'm taking advice from a door?!

DOOR: I told you, better get used to strange things from here on out!

ALICE: Oh well! *(takes a bite)* It's yummy! *(grows taller by standing on tiptoes or a step stool)* Curiouser and Curiouser! I'm huge! *(cries)*

(enter WHITE RABBIT)

WHITE RABBIT: I'm late! I'm late! Oh, the Queen will be savage if I've kept her waiting! *(sees ALICE)* AHH! GIANT! *(drops gloves and fan; exits)*

ALICE: Wait! I'm not a giant! I'm Alice. *(cries and fans herself with fan; then "shrinks")* Oh, I'm shrinking!

DOOR: You're tiny now. Watch out, you've made a big pool of water with those giant tears!

ALICE: I made a what? Whoa! SPLASH! Now I can swim through the door!

(ALL exit "swimming")

ACT 1 SCENE 3

(ALICE enters "swimming")

ALICE: I wish I hadn't cried so much, I'm all wet! *(MOUSE swims by)* A mouse! O' Mouse! *(MOUSE ignores her)* HEY MOUSE! Maybe he doesn't understand English. Perhaps he's French? Ou' est ma chatte?

MOUSE: Did you just ask me where your CAT is?!

ALICE: Sorry, that's all the French I know. Are you afraid of cats?

MOUSE: I'm a mouse! Would you like cats if you were me?

ALICE: I love cats! My cat Dinah is the best. She's so fluffy and great at catching mice.

MOUSE: Mice? Nice. I'm outta here!

ALICE: Oh, sorry. I won't talk about Dinah anymore. Do you like dogs? My neighbor has a wonderful dog. He catches all the rodents!

MOUSE: Do you not see that I'm a mouse? Humph! *(exits)*

ALICE: Touchy, touchy... Wait! Come back! *(exits saying...)* Let me tell you about snakes!

ACT 1 SCENE 4

(enter DODO)

DODO: What happened? I'm soaked! Good thing I'm back on dry land.

(enter MOUSE and ALICE)

ALICE: Please do come back! We won't talk about cats or dogs either if you don't like them!

DODO: I say, you're dripping wet. Did you get caught in the pool, too?

MOUSE: Yes. I'm soaked.

DODO: *(to ALICE)* Are you okay, dear?

ALICE: Well, I'd be better if I were dry and… *(looking around)* I just realized I'm talking to a mouse and a dodo? Everything is so confusing here! Wherever here is!

DODO: Who you calling a dodo?

ALICE: You. Dodo bird.

DODO: Oh, yeah.

MOUSE: I've got it! I'll tell you all the driest thing I know. William the Conqueror, whose cause was favoured by the pope…

DODO: UGH!

ALICE: Not again! That's the wrong kind of dry.

DODO: In that case, we'll try energetic matters.

MOUSE: Huh? I don't understand. *(points at audience)* And I don't think they understand. Especially that guy.

DODO: The best thing to get us dry is a caucus race.

ALICE: A WHAT?!

MOUSE: No wonder you're extinct!

DODO: What?!

MOUSE: Nothing! Go on!

DODO: You'll see. Follow me. *(ALL run around)* All done. Questions?

MOUSE: Who won?

DODO: You're all dry so everybody has won!

ALICE: This is so confusing!

MOUSE: You really are a dodo. Alice, I'd like to explain why I'm frightened of cats and dogs. *(melodramatically)* My tale is a long and sad one.

ALICE: *(looking at his tail)* It IS a long tail, but why do you call it sad?

MOUSE: My tale. My story. Not my tail!

ALICE: You have a knot in your tail? Let me help to undo it!

MOUSE: Ugh! You're not listening! I'm going to take my tale and my tail and go! *(exits holding tail)*

ALICE: Oh, he keeps running off. I wish Dinah were here to fetch him!

DODO: Who's Dinah, dear?

ALICE: My cat! She's great at catching mice and birds, too! Why she'll eat a bird as soon as look at it!

(DODO gasps and runs offstage)

ALICE: I wish I hadn't mentioned Dinah! *(exits)*

ACT 2 SCENE 1

(ALICE enters)

ALICE: Oh look! A little house that says White Rabbit on the door. This must be where he lives. *(knocks)* Oh, Rabbit! Hey, the door's open. *(exits; returns with bottle; to audience)* I didn't find the rabbit, but I found another bottle that says "Drink Me." Of course, I'm going to, because something interesting is sure to happen! *(she drinks and DODO enters placing a "roof" on her head and "walls" with window/armholes on each arm)* Uh oh!

(WHITE RABBIT enters)

WHITE RABBIT: What's happened to my house?!

DODO: What do you mean?

WHITE RABBIT: Just look at it, Dodo! There are giant arms and legs sticking out of it!

DODO: Cool.

WHITE RABBIT: Get an axe and chop them off for me.

DODO: That's gross. It's your house, you do it!

(ALICE swipes at them)

WHITE RABBIT and DODO: EEK!!

DODO: WHOA!!! Your house is NOT friendly!

WHITE RABBIT: We have to get it out. I guess there's only one thing left to do.

ALICE: *(to audience)* If they had any sense, they'd take the roof off.

DODO: Take the roof off?

WHITE RABBIT: NO! We must burn the house down.

ALICE: Burn?! I said take the roof off!! *(in a deep voice)* If you do, I'll set Dinah at you!

DODO and WHITE RABBIT: AHHH!!!

DODO: Here, throw these at it! *(gives "pebbles" to WHITE RABBIT; they throw them at ALICE)*

ALICE: OUCH! *(catches some)* Hey! This is cake! Chocolate, delicious, cake! *(eats it and removes house pieces)* I'm smaller now. I can get away! *(exits)*

DODO: Should we chase it?

WHITE RABBIT: No, let it go. I have my house back. *(picks up house pieces)* Tea, Dodo?

DODO: Sounds wonderful!

WHITE RABBIT: *(looks at watch)* Oops, I'm still late! *(runs offstage)*

DODO: Strange rabbit...

(DODO exits)

ACT 2 SCENE 2

(BLUE CATERPILLAR and ALICE enter)

ALICE: You're a blue caterpillar.

BLUE CATERPILLAR: Smart girl. Who are YOU?

ALICE: That's a hard question. I know who I WAS this morning, but I've changed several times since then.

BLUE CATERPILLAR: Explain yourself!

ALICE: Every time I eat or drink, I change size. It's awfully confusing! I'm lucky this dress has an elastic waistband.

BLUE CATERPILLAR: No, it's not.

ALICE: Just wait until you change from a caterpillar into a butterfly. Then, you'll see how strange it is!

BLUE CATERPILLAR: Butterfly? I don't understand. Now, who are YOU?

ALICE: Tell me who YOU are first!

BLUE CATERPILLAR: Why?

ALICE: Ugh! I'm leaving! *(walks away)*

BLUE CATERPILLAR: Wait! Don't go!

ALICE: Why?

BLUE CATERPILLAR: What size do you want to be?

ALICE: I'd like to be a little larger. Being three inches tall is miserable! I mean, I'm talking to a caterpillar.

BLUE CATERPILLAR: Hey! I'm three inches tall!

ALICE: Sorry!

BLUE CATERPILLAR: Listen, I have to leave, but if you eat from one side of my mushroom you'll grow, and if you eat from the other, you'll shrink. *(starts to leave)*

ALICE: WAIT! Which side is which?

BLUE CATERPILLAR: I forget. But remember, eating and drinking random things won't always solve your problems. Bye! *(exits)*

ALICE: *(mocks CATERPILLAR)* I forget, blah, blah, blah, blah, blah... I guess I'll take a piece of each. *(takes a bite of one piece and "grows")* Yes! I'm getting bigger!

(exits)

ACT 2 SCENE 3

(ALICE and CHESHIRE CAT enter; ALICE sees his big grin)

ALICE: *(to audience)* Do you see that? I didn't know cats COULD grin.

CHESHIRE CAT: We can and most of us do. It's because I'm a Cheshire cat.

ALICE: Cheshire cat!? You can grin AND talk!?

CHESHIRE CAT: Among other things.

ALICE: Awesome! Can you tell me which way to go?

CHESHIRE CAT: Where do you want to go?

ALICE: I don't care.

CHESHIRE CAT: Then, it doesn't matter.

ALICE: Well, I want to go SOMEWHERE!

CHESHIRE CAT: You're sure to get somewhere if you walk long enough.

ALICE: Ugh! So, you're a PHILOSOPHICAL, grinning, talking cat?

CHESHIRE CAT: Listen, the Hatter lives that way and the March Hare lives this way visit either you like, they're both mad.

ALICE: I don't want to be around mad people!

CHESHIRE CAT: We're all mad here. I'm mad. You're mad.

ALICE: I'M not mad!

CHESHIRE CAT: Are you here?

ALICE: Well, yes...

CHESHIRE CAT: Then, you have to be mad!

ALICE: How do you know you're mad?

CHESHIRE CAT: Think of a dog.

ALICE: Okay.

CHESHIRE CAT: When a dog's happy it wags its tail and when it's mad it growls. Well, when I'm angry I wag my tail and when I'm happy I growl. Therefore, I'm mad! See? *(purrs)*

ALICE: No. Anyway, you're purring, not growling.

CHESHIRE CAT: Hmmm, agree to disagree. Are you playing croquet with the Queen?

ALICE: I haven't been invited, yet.

CHESHIRE CAT: I'll see you there! *("vanishes" by putting on cloak)*

ALICE: Where did you go? *(CHESHIRE "reappears" by removing cloak)* AHHH, don't do that!!

CHESHIRE CAT: Which way will you go?

ALICE: I don't know.

CHESHIRE CAT: Hmmm... Not sure where that is. *("vanishes" again; ALICE walks across stage; CHESHIRE "reappears" behind her)* Did you say know or go?

ALICE: Ah!! Will you stop doing that?!

CHESHIRE CAT: Sorry! *(slowly pulls on the cloak to disappear until only a grin is visible)* Is that better?

ALICE: Barely. *(to audience)* I've often seen a cat without a grin, but a grin without a cat. It's most curious!

CHESHIRE CAT: Bye-bye...

(ALL exit)

ACT 2 SCENE 4

(MARCH HARE and MAD HATTER enter and sit)

MAD HATTER: A very merry unbirthday to you, March Hare!

MARCH HARE: What?

MAD HATTER: It's not your birthday, so it's your UNbirthday!

MARCH HARE: Um, that's from the sequel. Not this book!

MAD HATTER: There's another book?

MARCH HARE: Yes, next time Alice goes through the looking glass.

MAD HATTER: Spoiler alert!

MARCH HARE: It's NOT. That's the title of the sequel!

MAD HATTER: Very strange! I love it!

(ALICE enters and sits)

ALL: No room! No room!

ALICE: Nonsense, there's plenty of room.

MAD HATTER: So, you're not going to leave?

ALICE: Nope.

MARCH HARE: Okay. Have some soda.

ALICE: *(looks)* I don't see any.

MARCH HARE: That's because there isn't any!

(ALL but ALICE laugh)

ALICE: Then it was very rude of you to offer!

MARCH HARE: Just like it was very rude of you to sit when you weren't invited.

MAD HATTER: Oooh! Burn!

ALICE: Fine, I'll go.

MAD HATTER: Wait! Why is a raven like a writing desk?

ALICE: I have no idea.

MAD HATTER: I don't know either! *(He and MARCH HARE laugh)*

ALICE: They're both mad. I don't have time for this!

MAD HATTER: If you knew Time as well as I do, you wouldn't talk about wasting IT. It's HIM.

ALICE: WHAT?! You guys are crazy! I'm going! *(walks across stage)*

MARCH HARE: About time! *(ALL but ALICE laugh)*

ALICE: Humph! Look! That tree has a door. *(opens door)* Why it's the garden I've been looking for since scene two! I'm leaving this looney bin!

MAD HATTER: Oh, please! Don't go away MAD! *(ALL but ALICE laugh)*

(ALL exit)

ACT 3 SCENE 1

(CARD SOLDIER enters and "paints"; ALICE enters)

ALICE: *(to SOLDIER)* Why are you painting those roses?

SOLDIER: Shhh! Keep it down! She'll hear you.

ALICE: Who?

SOLDIER: The Queen of Hearts. She asked for red roses and I put in white by mistake. If she finds out, it's *(mocking queen)* off with my head!

ALICE: That's pretty violent for a children's book!

SOLDIER: Lewis Carroll thought children's books were boring without REAL danger. So, he created our murderous Queen. A fantastic villain if you ask me.

(enter WHITE RABBIT, QUEEN OF HEARTS, and KNAVE of HEARTS)

WHITE RABBIT: All bow to the Queen!

(ALL do except SOLDIER who tries to hide)

QUEEN: What's your name, child?

ALICE: My name is Alice, your majesty.

QUEEN: And who is this? *(pointing at SOLDIER)*

SOLDIER: *(stands and bows)* Your majesty!

QUEEN: What HAVE you been doing here?

SOLDIER: I planted white roses by mistake. I'm painting them red to fix it!

QUEEN: Humph! I'll fix you! Off with your head!

(SOLDIER melodramatically sobs as the QUEEN walks away)

ALICE: WHAT?!... Shhh! You shan't be beheaded. Go hide.

SOLDIER: Thank you!!!

(SOLDIER exits)

QUEEN: Alice! Come play croquet with us.

ALICE: Okay.

WHITE RABBIT: You'll need these. *(gives her a flamingo and a hedgehog)*

ALICE: A flamingo and a hedgehog? How am I supposed to play with these?

WHITE RABBIT: Like this! *(whacks ball; QUEEN sees ball fly; RABBIT points and blames audience member)*

QUEEN: *(pointing at random audience members)* You hit the ball too hard, off with your head! You haven't hit the ball at all, off with YOUR head! And your head looks like a ball. Disturbing. Off with all their heads!

KNAVE: Your Majesty, if you keep doing that we won't have an audience. *(QUEEN growls at KNAVE)* Nevermind, keep executing! *(to audience)* Sorry, but I want to keep MY head!

(CHESHIRE CAT enters only his head is visible behind ALICE)

CHESHIRE CAT: BOO!!!

ALICE: Ahh!! Stop doing that!

CHESHIRE CAT: Sorry! How do you like the Queen?

ALICE: I don't. Not at all!

KNAVE: *(to ALICE)* Who's that?

ALICE: My friend, the Cheshire Cat.

KNAVE: I don't like the look of it at all. However, it may kiss my hand if it likes.

CHESHIRE CAT: I'd rather not.

KNAVE: *(to QUEEN)* This cat's being mean. Make it go away!

QUEEN: Off with its head!

KNAVE: Hah! Oh, Executioner!

(SOLDIER enters)

SOLDIER: Yes, Knave?

KNAVE: *(points at CHESHIRE)* You know what to do.

SOLDIER: Hmmm... *(walks around CHESHIRE)* I can't cut off a head unless there's a body to cut it off from.

KNAVE: Nonsense! Anything that has a head can be beheaded!

QUEEN: If something's not done soon, you'll ALL lose your heads!

ALICE: You'd better ask the cat's owner. She went that way. *(points offstage)*

QUEEN: *(to SOLDIER)* Fetch her!

SOLDIER: Yes, your majesty! *(exits)*

ALICE: *(to CHESHIRE)* Go! Now!

(CHESHIRE CAT "vanishes")

KNAVE: Hey! Where did it go? *(starts looking around)* Here kitty, kitty!

WHITE RABBIT: *(to QUEEN)* Are you all right, my Queen?

QUEEN: No, I'm hungry! Knave. Bring me a tart!

(KNAVE exits and returns)

KNAVE: They're gone, your Majesty.

QUEEN: *(to KNAVE)* YOU ate my tarts! Off with everyone's head!

KNAVE: Mine too?!

QUEEN: No, you'll go to trial first. Seize him!

(SOLDIER enters and removes KNAVE; QUEEN and ALICE exit)

WHITE RABBIT: *(to audience)* Shhh... I'm sure you're all pardoned. She wouldn't have subjects to rule otherwise!

(WHITE RABBIT exits)

ACT 3 SCENE 2

(QUEEN, WHITE RABBIT, MAD HATTER, MARCH HARE, and ALICE enter then SOLDIER and KNAVE enter)

QUEEN: Read the charges.

WHITE RABBIT: The Queen of Hearts, she made some tarts, All on a summer day; The Knave of Hearts, he stole those tarts, And took them quite away!

QUEEN: Jurors what's your verdict?

WHITE RABBIT: Not yet, your Majesty!

QUEEN: Fine! Call your first witness.

WHITE RABBIT: FIRST WITNESS!!!

(MAD HATTER steps forward)

MAD HATTER: That's me, your Honor. I'm a hatter.

QUEEN: Give your evidence. Don't be nervous, or I'll have you executed on the spot.

MAD HATTER: *(nervously)* Me? Nervous? I'm not nervous! *(to audience)* Do I look like I'm nervous? *(QUEEN growls)* I am a poor man, your Majesty!

QUEEN: You're a poor speaker! Dismissed.

MAD HATTER: Thank you!

QUEEN: Off with his head!

MAD HATTER: WHAT?! *(runs offstage screaming madly; SOLDIER chases HATTER, then returns)*

WHITE RABBIT: SECOND WITNESS!!

(MARCH HARE steps up with pepper, ALL sneeze)

QUEEN: What are the tarts made of?

MARCH HARE: Pepper, mostly and molasses.

QUEEN: How would you know? The poem said I made the tarts. Behead that Hare!

MARCH HARE: NO!!! *(runs offstage screaming madly; SOLDIER chases MARCH HARE, then returns)*

WHITE RABBIT: THIRD WITNESS!! Alice!

QUEEN: What do you know of this?

ALICE: Nothing, whatever!

WHITE RABBIT: Then, it's time for the verdict!

QUEEN: NO, NO!! Sentence first—verdict afterwards.

ALICE: That makes no sense!

QUEEN: Hold your tongue!

ALICE: NO!!!

QUEEN: OFF WITH HER HEAD!!!

ALICE: Off with my WHAT!?!? *(turns to face them)* Wait! I'm not afraid of you. You're nothing but a pack of cards!

ALL: GET HER!!!

ALICE: Ahhh!!! I just wish I was little again!!!

(ALICE exits running; ALL exit chasing her)

ACT 3 SCENE 3

(ALICE enters and sleeps)

ALICE: *(talking in sleep)* I'm not afraid... nothing but... cards! *(wakes)* I've had such a curious dream! I followed a white rabbit down a hole and ended up in the strangest land where I kept changing size. I met a grinning cat and a wicked queen. What an adventure! It was a wonderland! I'll always remember you, Wonderland. See you in my dreams! *(yawns and starts to doze)*

WHITE RABBIT: *(runs across stage)* I'm late! I'm late!

ALICE: Here we go again! *(chases WHITE RABBIT offstage)*

THE END

The 20-Minute or so Alice's Adventures in Wonderland

By Lewis Carroll
Creatively modified by
Angela M. Herrick & Brendan P. Kelso

10 - 16 Actors

CAST OF CHARACTERS:

ALICE: a seriously confused little girl
¹SISTER: Alice's older sister
WHITE RABBIT: he's always late!
²DOOR: a Door, yes, a talking door!
³MOUSE: a mouse with a sad tale or is it tail?
⁴DODO: a wise bird
⁵DUCK: a kind duck
¹BLUE CATERPILLAR: a rude but helpful caterpillar
CHESHIRE CAT: a grinning and vanishing cat
MAD HATTER: mad maker of hats, likes tea
⁵MARCH HARE: friends with Hatter; also mad
QUEEN OF HEARTS: our wicked villain
²KING OF HEARTS: Queen's husband
³KNAVE OF HEARTS: works for the Queen
⁴EXECUTIONER: works for the Queen; very busy!
¹CARD SOLDIER: works in the Queen's garden

Additional actors can be **ANIMALS** and **CARD SOLDIERS**. Three different sized actors can play **ALICE** as she changes size.

The same actors can play the following parts:
[1]**SISTER, BLUE CATERPILLAR,** and **CARD SOLDIER**
[2]**DOOR** and **KING**
[3]**MOUSE** and **KNAVE**
[4]**DODO** and **EXECUTIONER**
[5]**DUCK** and **MARCH HARE**

ACT 1 SCENE 1

(enter ALICE and SISTER with book)

SISTER: Alice, time for your history lesson.

ALICE: No, it's soooo boring! What's the use of a book without pictures or conversations or tales of far off adventures?!

SISTER: Silly, girl. Don't you want to be smart like me?

ALICE: Like YOU? I'm not so sure! Kidding! I wish I was BIG like you, so wouldn't have to do this boring stuff!

SISTER: Just sit and listen. *(SISTER reads)* William the Conqueror, whose cause was favoured by the pope... blah, blah, blah...

(ALICE dozes; enter WHITE RABBIT; exit SISTER and ALICE wakes)

WHITE RABBIT: I'm late! I'm late! *(looks at watch)* Oh no! So LATE!!!

ALICE: Wow! A talking rabbit! Now, THAT'S something you don't see every day! *(WHITE RABBIT runs around and ALICE chases him; RABBIT exits)* He went down that deep, dark hole. I'm going in! What could possibly go wrong?! *(to audience)* This could be a HARE-raising adventure. Come on! *(exits)* AHHH!!!

ALICE: *(offstage)* I'mmmm stilllllll faaaaaaaliiiiiiiiing! AHHH!!!

ACT 1 SCENE 2

(ALICE and DOOR enter)

DOOR: Open me! Open me!

ALICE: Who said that?

DOOR: Down here!

ALICE: You're a talking door!?

DOOR: Yep! You are going to find A LOT of strange things in the next 15 minutes! Get used to it!!

(ALICE tries to open DOOR)

ALICE: You're locked. Knock-knock.

DOOR: Seriously? A knock-knock joke? Because I'm a door, right? Hilarious.

ALICE: I thought you'd be OPEN to a good joke. No? Then let me in!!

DOOR: Fine! My key's on the table.

(ALICE gets key and "opens" DOOR)

ALICE: It's the loveliest garden ever! Oh, no! I'm too big to get through. *(returns to table; sets key down)* Hmmm, there's a bottle that says "Drink Me."

DOOR: Definitely do that!

ALICE: What if it's poison?

DOOR: You're the main character and the play just started. Probably not poison.

ALICE: Good point! OK, bottoms up! *(drinks and gets down on knees)* Hey! I shrank to the right size! *(tries to open the door)* You've locked again?!

DOOR: Where's my key?... Whoops, you left it on the table!

ALICE: Ah, man.

DOOR: Hey, look there's some cake with a note.

ALICE: Oh, I like cake! *(picks it up)* It says, "Eat me."

DOOR: Maybe it'll help you grow. If it doesn't, you still get to eat cake!

ALICE: Good point, Door! *(to audience)* Wait. I'm taking advice from a door?!

DOOR: I told you, better get used to strange things from here on out!

ALICE: Oh well! *(takes a bite)* It's yummy! *(grows taller by standing on tiptoes or a step stool)* Curiouser and Curiouser! I'm huge! *(cries)*

(enter WHITE RABBIT)

WHITE RABBIT: I'm late! I'm late! Oh, the Queen will be savage if I've kept her waiting! *(sees ALICE)* AHH! GIANT! *(drops gloves and fan; exits)*

ALICE: Wait! I'm not a giant! I'm Alice. *(cries and fans herself with fan; then "shrinks")* Oh, I'm shrinking!

DOOR: You're tiny now. Watch out, you've made a big pool of water with those giant tears!

ALICE: I made a what? Whoa! SPLASH!

(ALL exit "swimming")

ACT 1 SCENE 3

(ALICE enters "swimming")

ALICE: I wish I hadn't cried so much, I'm all wet! *(MOUSE swims by)* A mouse! O' Mouse! *(MOUSE ignores her)* HEY MOUSE! Maybe he doesn't understand English. Perhaps he's French? Ou' est ma chatte?

MOUSE: Did you just ask me where your CAT is?!

ALICE: Sorry, that's all the French I know. Are you afraid of cats?

MOUSE: I'm a mouse! Would you like cats if you were me?

ALICE: I love cats! My cat Dinah is the best. I love the way she purrs, and she's great at catching mice.

MOUSE: Mice? Nice. I'm outta here!

ALICE: Oh, I beg your pardon. I won't talk about Dinah anymore. Do you like dogs? Our neighbor has a wonderful dog. He catches all the rodents!

MOUSE: Do you not see that I'm a mouse? Humph! *(exits)*

ALICE: Touchy, touchy... Wait! Come back! *(exits saying...)* Let me tell you about snakes!

ACT 1 SCENE 4

(enter DODO and DUCK)

DODO: Where did all the water come from? I'm soaked!

DUCK: There, there. We're back on dry land.

(enter MOUSE and ALICE)

ALICE: Please do come back! We won't talk about cats or dogs either if you don't like them!

DODO: I say, you're dripping wet. Did you get caught in the pool, too?

MOUSE: Yes. I'm soaked. It's awful.

DUCK: *(to ALICE)* Are you okay, dear?

ALICE: Well, I'd be better if I were dry and... *(looking around)* I just realized I'm talking to a mouse, a duck, and a dodo? Everything is so confusing here! Wherever here is!

DODO: Who you calling a dodo?

ALICE: You. Dodo bird.

DODO: Oh, yeah.

MOUSE: I've got it! You want dry, then I'll tell you all the driest thing I know. William the Conqueror, whose cause was favoured by the pope...

ALL: UGH!

ALICE: Not again! That's the wrong kind of dry.

DODO: In that case, we'll try energetic matters.

MOUSE: Huh? I don't understand.

DUCK: Me neither! *(points at audience)* And I don't think they understand. Especially that guy.

DODO: The best thing to get us dry is a caucus race.

ALL: A WHAT?!

DUCK: No wonder you're extinct!

DODO: What?!

DUCK: Nothing! Go on!

DODO: You'll see. Follow me. *(ALL run around)* All done. Questions?

DUCK: Who won?

DODO: You're all dry so everybody has won!

ALICE: What? This is so confusing!

DUCK: You really are a dodo.

MOUSE: Alice, I'd like to explain why I'm frightened of cats and dogs. Gather round. *(melodramatically)* My tale is a long and sad one.

ALICE: *(looking at his tail)* It IS a long tail, but why do you call it sad?

MOUSE: My tale. My story. Not my tail!

ALICE: You have a knot in your tail? Let me help to undo it!

MOUSE: Ugh! You're not listening! I'm going to take my tale and my tail and go! *(exits holding tail)*

ALICE: Oh, he keeps running off. I wish Dinah were here to fetch him!

DUCK: Who's Dinah, dear?

ALICE: My cat! She's great at catching mice and birds, too! Why she'll eat a bird as soon as look at it!

(ALL gasp and start to leave ALICE)

DODO: Ha! Who's the dodo now?

(ALL exit except ALICE)

ALICE: I wish I hadn't mentioned Dinah!

(exits)

ACT 2 SCENE 1

(WHITE RABBIT enters)

WHITE RABBIT: I'm STILL late! I'm late, and now I've lost my gloves. *(ALICE enters)* Why, Mary Ann, what are you doing out here? Run home this moment and fetch me a pair of gloves!

ALICE: Hey! That's not my name!

WHITE RABBIT: It doesn't matter! All servant girls are called Mary Ann in 19th century England.

ALICE: Ahh, first of all, I'm not your servant! Secondly, this is not England. And as far as I can, tell there are no rules here.

WHITE RABBIT: Fetch my gloves, NOW, Mary Ann!

ALICE: Okay! Okay! *(to audience)* I should get Dinah to take care of this one! *(WHITE RABBIT exits; ALICE walks across stage)* Here's a little house that says White Rabbit on the door. This must be it. *(exits; returns with bottle; to audience)* I found another bottle that says "Drink Me." Of course, I'm going to, because something interesting is sure to happen! *(she drinks and DODO enters placing a "roof" on her head and "walls" with window/armholes on each arm)* Uh oh!

(WHITE RABBIT enters)

WHITE RABBIT: Mary Ann! Mary Ann! You'd better fetch me those gloves. What's happened to my house?!

DODO: What do you mean?

WHITE RABBIT: Just look at it, Dodo! There are giant arms and legs sticking out of it!

DODO: Cool.

WHITE RABBIT: Get an axe and chop them off for me.

DODO: That's gross. It's your house, you do it!

(ALICE swipes at them)

WHITE RABBIT and DODO: EEK!!

DODO: WHOA!!! Your house is NOT friendly!

WHITE RABBIT: We have to get it out. I guess there's only one thing left to do.

ALICE: *(to audience)* If they had any sense, they'd take the roof off.

DODO: Take the roof off?

WHITE RABBIT: NO! We must burn the house down.

ALICE: Burn?! I said take the roof off!! *(in a deep voice)* If you do, I'll set Dinah at you!

DODO and WHITE RABBIT: AHHH!!!

DODO: Here, throw these at it! *(gives "pebbles" to WHITE RABBIT; they throw them at ALICE)*

ALICE: OUCH! *(catches some)* Hey! This is cake! Chocolate, delicious, cake! *(eats it and removes house pieces)* I'm smaller now. I can get away! *(exits)*

DODO: There it goes! Should we chase it?

WHITE RABBIT: No, let it go. I have my house back. *(picks up house pieces)* Tea, Dodo?

DODO: Sounds wonderful!

WHITE RABBIT: *(looks at watch)* Oops, I'm still late! *(runs offstage)*

DODO: Strange rabbit...

(DODO exits)

ACT 2 SCENE 2

(BLUE CATERPILLAR and ALICE enter)

ALICE: You're a blue caterpillar.

BLUE CATERPILLAR: Smart girl. Who are YOU?

ALICE: That's a hard question. I know who I WAS this morning, but I've changed several times since then.

BLUE CATERPILLAR: Explain yourself!

ALICE: Every time I eat or drink, I change size. It's awfully confusing! I'm lucky this dress has an elastic waistband.

BLUE CATERPILLAR: No, it's not.

ALICE: Just wait until you change from a caterpillar into a butterfly. Then, you'll see how strange it is!

BLUE CATERPILLAR: Butterfly? I don't understand. Now, who are YOU?

ALICE: Tell me who YOU are first!

BLUE CATERPILLAR: Why?

ALICE: Ugh! I'm leaving! *(walks away)*

BLUE CATERPILLAR: Wait! Don't go!

ALICE: Why?

BLUE CATERPILLAR: What size do you want to be?

ALICE: I'd like to be a little larger. Being three inches tall is miserable! I mean, I'm talking to a caterpillar.

BLUE CATERPILLAR: Hey! I'm three inches tall!

ALICE: Sorry!

BLUE CATERPILLAR: Listen, I have to leave, but if you eat from one side of my mushroom you'll grow, and if you eat from the other, you'll shrink. *(starts to leave)*

ALICE: WAIT! Which side is which?

BLUE CATERPILLAR: I forget. But remember, eating and drinking random things won't always solve your problems. Bye! *(exits)*

ALICE: *(mocks CATERPILLAR)* I forget, blah, blah, blah, blah, blah... I guess I'll take a piece of each. *(takes a bite of one piece and "grows")* Yes! I'm getting bigger!

(exits)

ACT 2 SCENE 3

(ALICE and CHESHIRE CAT enter; ALICE sees his big grin)

ALICE: *(to audience)* Do you see that? I didn't know cats **COULD** grin.

CHESHIRE CAT: We can and most of us do. It's because I'm a Cheshire cat.

ALICE: Cheshire cat!? You can grin AND talk!?

CHESHIRE CAT: Among other things.

ALICE: Awesome! Can you tell me which way to go?

CHESHIRE CAT: Where do you want to go?

ALICE: I don't care.

CHESHIRE CAT: Then, it doesn't matter.

ALICE: Well, I want to go **SOMEWHERE!**

CHESHIRE CAT: You're sure to get somewhere if you walk long enough.

ALICE: Ugh! So, you're a PHILOSOPHICAL, grinning, talking cat?

CHESHIRE CAT: Listen, the Hatter lives that way and the March Hare lives this way visit either you like, they're both mad.

ALICE: I don't want to be around mad people!

CHESHIRE CAT: We're all mad here. I'm mad. You're mad.

ALICE: I'M not mad!

CHESHIRE CAT: Are you here?

ALICE: Well, yes...

CHESHIRE CAT: Then, you have to be mad!

ALICE: How do you know you're mad?

CHESHIRE CAT: Think of a dog.

ALICE: Okay.

CHESHIRE CAT: When a dog's happy it wags its tail and when it's mad it growls. Well, when I'm angry I wag my tail and when I'm happy I growl. Therefore, I'm mad! See? *(purrs)*

ALICE: No. Anyway, you're purring, not growling.

CHESHIRE CAT: Hmmm, agree to disagree. Are you playing croquet with the Queen?

ALICE: I haven't been invited, yet.

CHESHIRE CAT: I'll see you there! *("vanishes" by putting on cloak)*

ALICE: Where did you go? *(CHESHIRE "reappears" by removing cloak)* AHHH, don't do that!!

CHESHIRE CAT: Which way will you go?

ALICE: I don't know.

CHESHIRE CAT: Hmmm... Not sure where that is. *("vanishes" again; ALICE walks across stage; CHESHIRE "reappears" behind her)* Did you say know or go?

ALICE: Ah!! Will you stop doing that?!

CHESHIRE CAT: Sorry! *(slowly pulls on the cloak to disappear until only a grin is visible)* Is that better?

ALICE: Barely. *(to audience)* I've often seen a cat without a grin, but a grin without a cat. It's most curious!

CHESHIRE CAT: Bye-bye...

(ALL exit)

ACT 2 SCENE 4

(MARCH HARE and MAD HATTER enter and sit)

MAD HATTER: A very merry unbirthday to you, March Hare!

MARCH HARE: What?

MAD HATTER: It's not your birthday, so it's your UNbirthday!

MARCH HARE: Um, that's from the sequel. Not this book!

MAD HATTER: There's another book?

MARCH HARE: Yes, next time Alice goes through the looking glass.

MAD HATTER: Spoiler alert!

MARCH HARE: It's NOT. That's the title of the sequel!

MAD HATTER: Very strange! I love it!

(ALICE enters and sits)

ALL: No room! No room!

ALICE: Nonsense, there's plenty of room.

MAD HATTER: So, you're not going to leave?

ALICE: Nope.

MARCH HARE: Okay. Have some soda.

ALICE: *(looks)* I don't see any.

MARCH HARE: That's because there isn't any!

(ALL but ALICE laugh)

ALICE: Then it was very rude of you to offer!

MARCH HARE: Just like it was very rude of you to sit when you weren't invited.

MAD HATTER: Ooooh! Burn!

ALICE: Fine, I'll go.

MAD HATTER: Wait! Why is a raven like a writing desk?

ALICE: I have no idea.

MAD HATTER: *(laughs)* I don't know either! *(laughs; HATTER looks at his watch)* Hey! What day of the month is it?

ALICE: It's the fourth.

MAD HATTER: Two days off! My watch is running slow. *(to MARCH HARE)* I told you buttering it wouldn't work!

MARCH HARE: *(takes watch)* I don't understand; it was the BEST butter!

MAD HATTER: You shouldn't have used a bread knife; it probably has crumbs in it now.

MARCH HARE: *(dips watch in teacup)* I don't understand. It was the BEST butter, you know.

ALICE: *(to audience)* Seriously, butter? They're both mad. I don't have time for this!

MAD HATTER: If you knew Time as well as I do, you wouldn't talk about wasting IT. It's HIM.

ALICE: WHAT?! You guys are crazy! I'm going! *(walks across stage)*

MARCH HARE: About TIME! *(ALL but ALICE laugh)*

ALICE: Humph! Look! That tree has a door. *(opens door)* Why it's the garden I've been looking for since scene two! I'm leaving this looney bin!

MAD HATTER: Oh, please! Don't go away MAD! *(ALL but ALICE laugh)*

(ALL exit)

ACT 3 SCENE 1

(CARD SOLDIER enters and "paints"; ALICE enters)

ALICE: *(to SOLDIER)* Why are you painting those roses?

SOLDIER: Shhh! Keep it down! She'll hear you.

ALICE: Who?

SOLDIER: The Queen of Hearts. She asked for red roses and I put in white by mistake. If she finds out, it's *(mocking queen)* off with my head!

ALICE: That's pretty violent for a children's book!

SOLDIER: Lewis Carroll thought children's books were boring without REAL danger. So, he created our murderous Queen. A fantastic villain if you ask me.

(enter WHITE RABBIT, QUEEN OF HEARTS, KING OF HEARTS, and KNAVE of HEARTS)

WHITE RABBIT: All bow to the Queen!

(ALL do except SOLDIER who tries to hide)

QUEEN: What's your name, child?

ALICE: My name is Alice, your majesty.

QUEEN: And who is this? *(pointing at SOLDIER)*

SOLDIER: *(stands and bows)* Your majesty!

QUEEN: What HAVE you been doing here?

SOLDIER: I planted white roses by mistake. I'm painting them red to fix it!

QUEEN: Humph! I'll fix you! Off with your head!

(SOLDIER melodramatically sobs as the QUEEN walks away)

ALICE: WHAT?!... Shhh! You shan't be beheaded. Go hide.

SOLDIER: Thank you!!!

(SOLDIER exits)

QUEEN: Alice! Come play croquet with us.

ALICE: Okay.

WHITE RABBIT: You'll need these. *(gives her a flamingo and a hedgehog)*

ALICE: A flamingo and a hedgehog? How am I supposed to play with these?

WHITE RABBIT: Like this! *(whacks ball; QUEEN sees ball fly; RABBIT points and blames audience member)*

QUEEN: *(pointing at random audience members)* You hit the ball too hard, off with your head! You haven't hit the ball at all, off with YOUR head! And your head looks like a ball. Disturbing. Off with all their heads!

KING: My dear, if you keep doing that we won't have an audience. *(QUEEN growls at KING)* Nevermind, keep executing! *(to audience)* Sorry, but I want to keep MY head!

(CHESHIRE CAT enters only his head is visible behind ALICE)

CHESHIRE CAT: BOO!!!

ALICE: Ahh!! Stop doing that!

CHESHIRE CAT: Sorry! How do you like the Queen?

ALICE: I don't. Not at all!

KING: *(to ALICE)* Who's that?

ALICE: My friend, the Cheshire Cat.

KING: I don't like the look of it at all. However, it may kiss my hand if it likes.

CHESHIRE CAT: I'd rather not.

KING: *(to QUEEN)* This cat's being mean. Make it go away!

QUEEN: Off with its head!

KING: Hah! Oh, Executioner!

(EXECUTIONER enters)

EXECUTIONER: You called?

KING: *(points at CHESHIRE)* You know what to do.

EXECUTIONER: Hmmm… *(walks around CHESHIRE)* I can't cut off a head unless there's a body to cut it off from.

KING: Nonsense! Anything that has a head can be beheaded!

QUEEN: If something's not done soon, you'll ALL lose your heads!

ALICE: You'd better ask the cat's owner. She went that way. *(points offstage)*

QUEEN: *(to EXECUTIONER)* Fetch her!

EXECUTIONER: Yes, your majesty! *(exits)*

ALICE: *(to CHESHIRE)* Go! Now!

(CHESHIRE CAT "vanishes")

KING: Hey! Where did it go?

ALL: Here kitty, kitty!

KING: *(to QUEEN)* Are you all right, dear?

QUEEN: No, I'm hungry! Knave, bring me a tart!

(KNAVE exits and returns)

KNAVE: They're gone, your Majesty.

QUEEN: *(to KNAVE)* YOU ate my tarts! Off with everyone's head!

KNAVE: Mine too?!

QUEEN: No, you'll go to trial first. Seize him!

(SOLDIERS enter and remove KNAVE; QUEEN, ALICE, and WHITE RABBIT exit)

KING: *(to audience)* Shhh... Don't worry. You're all pardoned. We wouldn't have subjects to rule otherwise!

(KING exits)

ACT 3 SCENE 2

(KING, QUEEN, WHITE RABBIT, MAD HATTER, MARCH HARE, ALICE, and ANIMALS enter; ANIMALS sit as if in a jury box; SOLDIER, KNAVE, and EXECUTIONER enter)

KING: Read the charges.

WHITE RABBIT: Where shall I begin?

KING: Begin at the beginning, and go on till you come to the end: then stop.

WHITE RABBIT: The Queen of Hearts, she made some tarts, All on a summer day: The Knave of Hearts, he stole those tarts, And took them quite away!

KING: Jurors what's your verdict?

WHITE RABBIT: Not yet, Sire!

KING: Fine! Call your first witness.

WHITE RABBIT: FIRST WITNESS!!!

(MAD HATTER steps forward)

MAD HATTER: That's me, your Honor. I'm a hatter.

KING: Give your evidence. Don't be nervous, or I'll have you executed on the spot.

MAD HATTER: *(nervously)* Me? Nervous? I'm not nervous! *(to audience)* Do I look like I'm nervous?

KING: Just give your evidence!

MAD HATTER: I am a poor man, your Majesty!

KING: You're a poor speaker! Dismissed.

MAD HATTER: Thank you!

KING: Off with his head!

MAD HATTER: WHAT?! *(runs offstage screaming madly; SOLDIER and EXECUTIONER chase HATTER, then return)*

QUEEN: Excuse me! That's MY line!

KING: Yes, dear!

WHITE RABBIT: SECOND WITNESS!!

(MARCH HARE steps up with pepper, ALL sneeze)

KING: What are the tarts made of?

MARCH HARE: Pepper, mostly and molasses.

QUEEN: How would you know? The poem said I made the tarts. Behead that Hare!

MARCH HARE: NO!!! *(runs offstage screaming madly; SOLDIER and EXECUTIONER chase MARCH HARE, then return)*

KING: ACHOO!!! *(to QUEEN)* Really, my dear, you must cross-examine the next witness. My head hurts!

QUEEN: Okay.

WHITE RABBIT: THIRD WITNESS!! Alice!

QUEEN: What do you know of this?

ALICE: Nothing, whatever!

QUEEN: Then, I call for a verdict!

ALICE: That makes no sense.

KING: Don't care. We want a verdict!

QUEEN: NO, NO!! Sentence first—verdict afterwards.

ALICE: But, you just said you wanted a verdict!

QUEEN: Hold your tongue!

ALICE: NO!!!

QUEEN: OFF WITH HER HEAD!!!

ALICE: Off with my WHAT!?!? *(turns to face them)* Wait! I'm not afraid of you. You're nothing but a pack of cards!

ALL: GET HER!!!

ALICE: Ahhh!!! I just wish I was little again!!!

(ALICE exits running; ALL exit chasing her)

ACT 3 SCENE 3

(ALICE and SISTER enter; ALICE sleeps)

ALICE: *(talking in sleep)* I'm not afraid... nothing but... cards!

SISTER: Alice, wake up!

ALICE: *(wakes)* I've had such a curious dream! I followed a white rabbit down a hole and ended up in the strangest land where I kept changing size. I also met a grinning cat and a wicked queen.

SISTER: It was a curious dream! Sounds like a wonderland.

ALICE: You're right! It was a wonderland! I'm going to get some tea and a pepper tart. Would you like one?

SISTER: A pepper tart? No thanks. *(ALICE exits)* I hope when Alice is a grown woman, she'll keep her sense of wonder and imagination. Maybe, if I think about Wonderland when I fall asleep, I can visit it in my dreams. *(falls asleep)*

WHITE RABBIT: *(runs across stage)* I'm late! I'm late!

SISTER: *(wakes)* How curious!

(SISTER chases WHITE RABBIT offstage)

THE END

The 25-Minute or so Alice's Adventures in Wonderland

By Lewis Carroll
Creatively modified by
Angela M. Herrick & Brendan P. Kelso

13 - 21+ Actors

CAST OF CHARACTERS:

ALICE: a seriously confused little girl
[1]SISTER: Alice's older sister
WHITE RABBIT: he's always late!
[2]DOOR: a Door, yes, a talking door!
[3]MOUSE: a mouse with a sad tale or is it tail?
[4]DODO: a wise bird
[5]EAGLET: baby eagle
[6]DUCK: a kind duck
[7]LIZARD BILL: White Rabbit's friend
[8]BLUE CATERPILLAR: a rude but helpful caterpillar
[5]COOK: cook who uses a LOT of pepper
CHESHIRE CAT: a grinning and vanishing cat
MAD HATTER: mad maker of hats, likes tea
[1]MARCH HARE: friends with Hatter; also mad
[3]DORMOUSE: a very sleepy mouse
[6]QUEEN OF HEARTS: our wicked villain
[7]KING OF HEARTS: Queen's husband
[2]KNAVE OF HEARTS: works for the Queen
[4]EXECUTIONER: works for the Queen; very busy!
[8]CARD SOLDIER 1: works in the Queen's garden
CARD SOLDIER 2: also works in the Queen's garden

Additional actors can be ANIMALS and CARD SOLDIERS. Three different sized actors can play ALICE as she changes size.

The same actors can play the following parts:
[1] SISTER and MARCH HARE
[2] DOOR and KNAVE
[3] MOUSE and DORMOUSE
[4] DODO and EXECUTIONER
[5] EAGLET and COOK
[6] DUCK and QUEEN
[7] LIZARD BILL and KING
[8] BLUE CATERPILLAR and a CARD SOLDIER

ACT 1 SCENE 1
Down the Rabbit Hole

(enter ALICE and SISTER with book)

SISTER: Alice, time for your history lesson.

ALICE: No, it's soooo boring! What's the use of a book without pictures or conversations or tales of far off adventures?!

SISTER: Silly, girl. Don't you want to be smart like me?

ALICE: Like YOU? I'm not so sure! Kidding! I wish I was BIG like you, so wouldn't have to do this boring stuff!

SISTER: Just sit and listen. *(SISTER reads)* William the Conqueror, whose cause was favoured by the pope... blah, blah, blah...

(ALICE dozes; enter WHITE RABBIT; exit SISTER and ALICE wakes)

WHITE RABBIT: I'm late! I'm late! *(looks at watch)* Oh no! So LATE!!!

ALICE: Wow! A talking rabbit! Now, THAT'S something you don't see every day! *(WHITE RABBIT runs around and ALICE chases him; RABBIT exits)* He went down that deep, dark hole. I'm going in! What could possibly go wrong?! *(to audience)* This could be a HARE-raising adventure. Come on! *(exits)* AHHH!!!

ALICE: *(offstage)* I'mmmm stillllll faaaaaaaliiiiiiiiing! AHHH!!!

ACT 1 SCENE 2

(ALICE and DOOR enter)

DOOR: Open me! Open me!

ALICE: Who said that?

DOOR: Down here!

ALICE: You're a talking door!?

DOOR: Yep! You are going to find A LOT of strange things in the next 15 minutes! Get used to it!!

(ALICE tries to open DOOR)

ALICE: You're locked. Knock-knock.

DOOR: Seriously? A knock-knock joke? Because I'm a door, right? Hilarious.

ALICE: I thought you'd be OPEN to a good joke. No? Then let me in!!

DOOR: Fine! My key's over there on the table.

(ALICE gets key and "opens" DOOR)

ALICE: It's the loveliest garden ever! Oh, no! I'm too big to get through. *(returns to table; sets key down)* Hmmm, there's a bottle that says "Drink Me."

DOOR: Definitely do that!

ALICE: What if it's poison?

DOOR: You're the main character and the play just started. Probably not poison.

ALICE: Good point! You're so a-DOOR-able! Get it?

DOOR: Yes, I'm a door. Drink!

ALICE: OK, bottoms up! *(drinks and gets down on knees)* Hey! I shrank to the right size! *(tries to open the door)* You've locked again?!

DOOR: Where's my key?... Whoops, you left it on the table!

ALICE: Ah, man.

DOOR: Hey, look there's some cake with a note.

ALICE: Oh, I like cake! *(picks it up)* It says, "Eat me."

DOOR: Maybe it'll help you grow. If it doesn't, you still get to eat cake!

ALICE: Good point, Door! *(aside to audience)* Wait. I'm taking advice from a door?!

DOOR: I told you, better get used to strange things from here on out!

ALICE: Oh well! *(takes a bite)* It's yummy! *(grows taller by standing on tiptoes or a step stool)* Curiouser and Curiouser! I'm huge! *(cries)*

(enter WHITE RABBIT)

WHITE RABBIT: I'm late! I'm late! Oh, the Queen will be savage if I've kept her waiting! *(sees ALICE)* AHH! GIANT! *(drops gloves and fan; exits)*

ALICE: Wait! I'm not a giant! I'm Alice. *(cries and fans herself with fan; then "shrinks")* Oh, I'm shrinking!

DOOR: You're tiny now. Watch out, you've made a big pool of water with those giant tears!

ALICE: I made a what? Whoa! SPLASH!

(ALL exit "swimming")

ACT 1 SCENE 3

The Pool of Tears

(ALICE enters "swimming")

ALICE: I wish I hadn't cried so much, I'm all wet! *(MOUSE swims by)* A mouse! O' Mouse! *(MOUSE ignores her)* HEY MOUSE! Maybe he doesn't understand English. Perhaps he's French? Où' est ma chatte?

MOUSE: Did you just ask me where your CAT is?!

ALICE: Sorry, that's all the French I know. Are you afraid of cats?

MOUSE: I'm a mouse! Would you like cats if you were me?

ALICE: I love cats! My cat Dinah is the best. I love the way she purrs, and she's great at catching mice.

MOUSE: Mice? Nice. I'm outta here!

ALICE: Oh, I beg your pardon. I won't talk about Dinah anymore. Do you like dogs? Our neighbor has a wonderful dog. He catches all the rodents!

MOUSE: Do you not see that I'm a mouse? Humph! *(exits)*

ALICE: Touchy, touchy... Wait! Come back! *(exits saying...)* Let me tell you about snakes!

ACT 1 SCENE 4
The Caucus Race and the Long Tale

(enter DODO, EAGLET, and DUCK)

DODO: Where did all the water come from? I'm soaked!

EAGLET: *(cries)* Me too!

DUCK: *(to EAGLET)* There, there. We're back on dry land.

(enter MOUSE and ALICE)

ALICE: Please do come back! We won't talk about cats or dogs either if you don't like them!

DODO: I say, you're dripping wet. Did you get caught in the pool, too?

MOUSE: Yes. I'm soaked. It's awful.

DUCK: *(to ALICE)* Are you okay, dear?

ALICE: Well, I'd be better if I were dry and... *(looking around)* I just realized I'm talking to a mouse, an eaglet, a duck, and a dodo? Everything is so confusing here! Wherever here is!

DODO: Who you calling a dodo?

ALICE: You. Dodo bird.

DODO: Oh, yeah.

MOUSE: I've got it! You want dry, then I'll tell you all the driest thing I know. William the Conqueror, whose cause was favoured by the pope...

ALL: UGH!

ALICE: Not again!

DUCK: Is everyone dry?

ALL: No!

EAGLET: That was the wrong kind of dry.

DODO: In that case, we'll try energetic matters.

EAGLET: Huh? I don't understand.

DUCK: Me neither! *(points at audience)* And I don't think they understand. Especially that guy.

DODO: The best thing to get us dry is a caucus race.

ALL: A WHAT?!

DUCK: No wonder you're extinct!

DODO: What?!

DUCK: Nothing! Go on!

DODO: You'll see. Follow me. *(ALL run around)* All done. Questions?

EAGLET: Who won?

DODO: You're all dry so everybody has won!

ALICE: What? This is so confusing!

DUCK: You really are a dodo.

MOUSE: Alice, I'd like to explain why I am so frightened of cats and dogs. Gather round. *(melodramatically)* My tale is a long and sad one.

ALICE: *(looking at his tail)* It IS a long tail, but why do you call it sad?

MOUSE: My tale. My story. Not my tail!

ALICE: You have a knot in your tail? Let me help to undo it!

MOUSE: Ugh! You're not listening! I'm going to take my tale and my tail and go! *(exits holding tail)*

ALICE: Oh, he keeps running off. I wish Dinah were here to fetch him!

DUCK: Who's Dinah, dear?

ALICE: My cat! She's great at catching mice.

EAGLET: She is?

ALICE: Yes, and birds, too! Why she'll eat a bird as soon as look at it!

(ALL gasp and start to leave ALICE)

DODO: Ha! Who's the dodo now?

(ALL exit except ALICE)

ALICE: I wish I hadn't mentioned Dinah!

(exits)

ACT 2 SCENE 1
The Rabbit Sends in Lizard Bill

(WHITE RABBIT enters)

WHITE RABBIT: I'm STILL late! I'm late, and now I've lost my gloves.

(ALICE enters)

WHITE RABBIT: Why, Mary Ann, what are you doing out here? Run home this moment and fetch me a pair of gloves!

ALICE: Hey! That's not my name!

WHITE RABBIT: It doesn't matter! All servant girls are called Mary Ann in 19th century England.

ALICE: Ahh, first of all, I'm not your servant! Secondly, this is not England. And as far as I can, tell there are no rules here.

WHITE RABBIT: Fetch my gloves, NOW, Mary Ann!

ALICE: Okay! Okay! *(to audience)* I should get Dinah to take care of this one! *(WHITE RABBIT exits; ALICE walks across stage)* Here's a little house that says White Rabbit on the door. This must be it. *(exits; returns with bottle; to audience)* I found another bottle that says "Drink Me." Of course, I'm going to, because something interesting is sure to happen! *(she drinks and DODO enters placing a "roof" on her head and "walls" with window/armholes on each arm)* Uh oh!

(WHITE RABBIT enters)

WHITE RABBIT: Mary Ann! Mary Ann! You'd better fetch me those gloves. What's happened to my house?!

DODO: What do you mean?

WHITE RABBIT: Just look at it, Dodo! There are giant arms and legs sticking out of it!

DODO: Cool.

WHITE RABBIT: Get an axe and chop them off for me.

DODO: That's gross. It's your house, you do it!

(ALICE swipes at them)

WHITE RABBIT and DODO: EEK!!

(Enter LIZARD BILL)

LIZARD BILL: What's the trouble, Boss?

WHITE RABBIT: Lizard Bill! Something giant has filled up my house. Climb down the chimney and see what it is.

LIZARD BILL: Okay, Boss. *(he moves toward ALICE's foot; she kicks at him; he runs to other side of stage)* WHOA!!! Your house grew arms and legs and it's NOT friendly!

WHITE RABBIT: We have to get it out. I guess there's only one thing left to do.

ALICE: *(to audience)* If they had any sense, they'd take the roof off.

LIZARD BILL: Take the roof off, Boss?

WHITE RABBIT: NO! We must burn the house down.

ALICE: Burn?! I said take the roof off!! *(in a deep voice)* If you do, I'll set Dinah at you!

ANIMALS: AHHH!!!

DODO: Here, throw these at it! *(gives "pebbles" to WHITE RABBIT and LIZARD BILL; they throw them at ALICE)*

ALICE: OUCH! *(catches some)* Hey! This is cake! Chocolate, delicious, cake! *(eats it and removes house pieces)* I'm smaller now. I can get away! *(exits)*

LIZARD BILL: There it goes! Should we chase it?

WHITE RABBIT: No, let it go. I have my house back. *(picks up house pieces)* Tea, gentlemen?

DODO: Sounds wonderful!

WHITE RABBIT: *(looks at watch)* Oops, I'm still late! *(runs offstage)*

LIZARD BILL: Strange little rabbit...

(ALL exit)

ACT 2 SCENE 2
Advice from a Caterpillar

(BLUE CATERPILLAR and ALICE enter)

ALICE: You're a blue caterpillar.

BLUE CATERPILLAR: Smart girl. Who are YOU?

ALICE: That's a hard question. I know who I WAS this morning, but I've changed several times since then.

BLUE CATERPILLAR: Explain yourself!

ALICE: Every time I eat or drink, I change size. It's awfully confusing! I'm lucky this dress has an elastic waistband.

BLUE CATERPILLAR: No, it's not.

ALICE: Just wait until you change from a caterpillar into a butterfly. Then, you'll see how strange it is!

BLUE CATERPILLAR: Butterfly? I don't understand. Now, who are YOU?

ALICE: Tell me who YOU are first!

BLUE CATERPILLAR: Why?

ALICE: Ugh! I'm leaving! *(walks away)*

BLUE CATERPILLAR: Wait! Don't go!

ALICE: Why?

BLUE CATERPILLAR: What size do you want to be?

ALICE: I'd like to be a little larger. Being three inches tall is miserable! I mean, I'm talking to a caterpillar.

BLUE CATERPILLAR: Hey! I'm three inches tall!

ALICE: Sorry!

BLUE CATERPILLAR: Listen, I have to leave, but if you eat from one side of my mushroom you'll grow, and if you eat from the other, you'll shrink. *(starts to leave)*

ALICE: WAIT! Which side is which?

BLUE CATERPILLAR: I forget. But remember, eating and drinking random things won't always solve your problems. Bye! *(exits)*

ALICE: *(mocks CATERPILLAR)* I forget, blah, blah, blah, blah, blah... I guess I'll take a piece of each. *(takes a bite of one piece and "grows")* Yes! I'm getting bigger!

(exits)

ACT 2 SCENE 3

(ALICE and CHESHIRE CAT enter; ALICE sees his big grin)

ALICE: *(to audience)* Do you see that? I didn't know cats COULD grin.

CHESHIRE CAT: We can and most of us do. It's because I'm a Cheshire cat.

ALICE: Cheshire cat!? You can grin AND talk!?

CHESHIRE CAT: Among other things.

ALICE: Awesome! Can you tell me which way to go?

CHESHIRE CAT: Where do you want to go?

ALICE: I don't care.

CHESHIRE CAT: Then, it doesn't matter.

ALICE: Well, I want to go SOMEWHERE!

CHESHIRE CAT: You're sure to get somewhere if you walk long enough.

ALICE: Ugh! So, you're a PHILOSOPHICAL, grinning, talking, cat?

CHESHIRE CAT: Listen, the Hatter lives that way and the March Hare lives this way visit either you like, they're both mad.

ALICE: I don't want to be around mad people!

CHESHIRE CAT: We're all mad here. I'm mad. You're mad.

ALICE: I'M not mad!

CHESHIRE CAT: Are you here?

ALICE: Well, yes...

CHESHIRE CAT: Then, you have to be mad!

ALICE: How do you know you're mad?

CHESHIRE CAT: Think of a dog.

ALICE: Okay.

CHESHIRE CAT: When a dog's happy it wags its tail and when it's mad it growls. Well, when I'm angry I wag my tail and when I'm happy I growl. Therefore, I'm mad! See? *(purrs)*

ALICE: No. Anyway, you're purring, not growling.

CHESHIRE CAT: Hmmm, agree to disagree. Are you playing croquet with the Queen?

ALICE: I haven't been invited, yet.

CHESHIRE CAT: I'll see you there! *("vanishes" by putting on cloak)*

ALICE: Where did you go? *(CHESHIRE "reappears" by removing cloak)* AHHH, don't do that!!

CHESHIRE CAT: Which way will you go?

ALICE: I don't know.

CHESHIRE CAT: Hmmm... Not sure where that is. *("vanishes" again; ALICE walks across stage; CHESHIRE "reappears" behind her)* Did you say know or go?

ALICE: Ah!! Will you stop doing that?!

CHESHIRE CAT: Sorry! *(slowly pulls on the cloak to disappear until only a grin is visible)* Is that better?

ALICE: Barely. *(to audience)* I've often seen a cat without a grin, but a grin without a cat. It's most curious!

CHESHIRE CAT: Bye-bye...

(ALL exit)

ACT 2 SCENE 4

A Mad Tea Party

(MARCH HARE, MAD HATTER, and DORMOUSE enter and sit; DORMOUSE dozes between the other two)

MAD HATTER: A very merry unbirthday to you, March Hare!

MARCH HARE: What?

MAD HATTER: It's not your birthday, so it's your UNbirthday!

MARCH HARE: Um, that's from the sequel. Not this book!

MAD HATTER: There's another book?

MARCH HARE: Yes, next time Alice goes through the looking glass.

DORMOUSE: Spoiler alert!

MARCH HARE: It's NOT. That's the title of the sequel!

MAD HATTER: Very strange! I love it!

(ALICE enters and sits)

ALL: No room! No room!

ALICE: Nonsense, there's plenty of room.

MAD HATTER: So, you're not going to leave?

ALICE: Nope.

MARCH HARE: Okay. Have some soda.

ALICE: *(looks)* I don't see any.

MARCH HARE: That's because there isn't any!

(ALL but ALICE laugh)

ALICE: Then it was very rude of you to offer!

MARCH HARE: Just like it was very rude of you to sit when you weren't invited.

DORMOUSE: Oooh! Burn!

ALICE: Fine, I'll go.

MAD HATTER: Wait! Why is a raven like a writing desk?

ALICE: I have no idea.

MAD HATTER: *(laughs)* I don't know either! *(ALL but ALICE laugh; HATTER looks at his watch)* Hey! What day of the month is it?

ALICE: It's the fourth.

MAD HATTER: Two days off! My watch is running slow. *(to MARCH HARE)* I told you buttering it wouldn't work!

MARCH HARE: *(takes watch)* I don't understand; it was the BEST butter!

MAD HATTER: You shouldn't have used a bread knife; it probably has crumbs in it now.

MARCH HARE: *(dips watch in teacup)* I don't understand. It was the BEST butter, you know.

ALICE: *(to audience)* Seriously, butter? They're both mad. I don't have time for this!

MAD HATTER: If you knew Time as well as I do, you wouldn't talk about wasting IT. It's HIM.

ALICE: WHAT?! You guys are crazy! I'm going! *(walks across stage)*

MARCH HARE: About TIME! *(ALL but ALICE laugh)*

ALICE: Humph! Look! That tree has a door. *(opens door)* Why it's the garden I've been looking for since scene two! I'm leaving this looney bin!

MAD HATTER: Oh, please! Don't go away MAD! *(ALL but ALICE laugh)*

(ALL exit)

ACT 3 SCENE 1

The Queen's Croquet-Ground

(CARD SOLDIERS enter and "paint"; ALICE enters)

ALICE: *(to SOLDIERS)* Why are you painting those roses?

SOLDIER 1: Shhh! Keep it down! She'll hear you.

ALICE: Who?

SOLDIER 2: The Queen of Hearts.

SOLDIER 1: She asked for red roses and we put in white by mistake. If she finds out, it's *(mocking queen)* off with our heads!

ALICE: That's pretty violent for a children's book!

SOLDIER 2: Lewis Carroll thought children's books were boring without REAL danger. So, he created our murderous Queen.

SOLDIER 1: A fantastic villain if you ask me.

(enter WHITE RABBIT, QUEEN OF HEARTS, KING OF HEARTS, and KNAVE of HEARTS)

WHITE RABBIT: All bow to the Queen!

(ALL do except SOLDIERS who try to hide)

QUEEN: What's your name, child?

ALICE: My name is Alice, your majesty.

QUEEN: And who are they? *(pointing at SOLDIERS)*

SOLDIERS: *(stand and bow)* Your majesty!

QUEEN: What HAVE you been doing here?

SOLDIER 1: We planted white roses by mistake.

SOLDIER 2: We painted them red to fix it!

QUEEN: Humph! I'll fix you! Off with their heads!

(SOLDIERS melodramatically sobs as the QUEEN walks away)

ALICE: WHAT?!... Shhh! You shan't be beheaded. Go hide.

SOLDIERS: Thank you!!!

(SOLDIERS exit)

QUEEN: Alice! Come play croquet with us.

ALICE: Okay.

WHITE RABBIT: You'll need these. *(gives her a flamingo and a hedgehog)*

ALICE: A flamingo and a hedgehog? How am I supposed to play with these?

WHITE RABBIT: Like this! *(whacks ball; QUEEN sees ball fly; RABBIT points and blames audience member)*

QUEEN: *(pointing at random audience members)* You hit the ball too hard, off with your head! You haven't hit the ball at all, off with YOUR head! And your head looks like a ball. Disturbing. Off with all their heads!

KING: My dear, if you do that we won't have an audience. *(QUEEN growls at KING)* Nevermind, keep executing! *(to audience)* Sorry, but I want to keep MY head!

(CHESHIRE CAT enters only his head is visible behind ALICE)

CHESHIRE CAT: BOO!!!

ALICE: Ahh!! Stop doing that!

CHESHIRE CAT: Sorry! How do you like the Queen?

ALICE: I don't. Not at all!

KING: *(to ALICE)* Who's that?

ALICE: My friend, the Cheshire Cat.

KING: I don't like the look of it at all. However, it may kiss my hand if it likes.

CHESHIRE CAT: I'd rather not.

KING: *(to QUEEN)* This cat's being mean. Make it go away!

QUEEN: Off with its head!

KING: Hah! Oh, Executioner!

(EXECUTIONER enters)

EXECUTIONER: You called?

KING: *(points at CHESHIRE)* You know what to do.

EXECUTIONER: Hmmm... *(walks around CHESHIRE)* I can't cut off a head unless there's a body to cut it off from.

KING: Nonsense! Anything that has a head can be beheaded!

QUEEN: If something's not done soon, you'll ALL lose your heads!

ALICE: You'd better ask the cat's owner. She went that way. *(points offstage)*

QUEEN: *(to EXECUTIONER)* Fetch her!

EXECUTIONER: Yes, your majesty! *(exits)*

ALICE: *(to CHESHIRE)* Go! Now!

(CHESHIRE CAT "vanishes")

KING: Hey! Where did it go?

ALL: Here kitty, kitty!

KING: *(to QUEEN)* Are you all right, dear?

QUEEN: No, I'm hungry! Knave, bring me a tart!

(KNAVE exits and returns)

KNAVE: They're gone, your Majesty.

QUEEN: *(to KNAVE)* YOU ate my tarts! Off with everyone's head!

KNAVE: Mine too?!

QUEEN: No, you'll go to trial first. Seize him!

(SOLDIERS enter and remove KNAVE; QUEEN, ALICE, and WHITE RABBIT exit)

KING: *(to audience)* Shhh... Don't worry. You're all pardoned. We wouldn't have subjects to rule otherwise!

(KING exits)

ACT 3 SCENE 2

Who Stole the Tarts?

Alice's Evidence

(KING, QUEEN, WHITE RABBIT, MAD HATTER, MARCH HARE, DORMOUSE, ALICE, and ANIMALS enter; ANIMALS sit as if in a jury box; SOLDIERS, KNAVE, and EXECUTIONER enter)

KING: Read the charges.

WHITE RABBIT: Where shall I begin?

KING: Begin at the beginning, and go on till you come to the end: then stop.

WHITE RABBIT: The Queen of Hearts, she made some tarts, All on a summer day: The Knave of Hearts, he stole those tarts, And took them quite away!

KING: Jurors what's your verdict?

WHITE RABBIT: Not yet, Sire!

KING: Fine! Call your first witness.

WHITE RABBIT: FIRST WITNESS!!!

MAD HATTER: That's me, your Honor. I'm a hatter.

KING: Give your evidence. Don't be nervous, or I'll have you executed on the spot.

MAD HATTER: *(nervously)* Me? Nervous? I'm not nervous! *(to audience)* Do I look like I'm nervous?

KING: Just give your evidence!

MAD HATTER: I am a poor man, your Majesty!

KING: You're a poor speaker! Dismissed.

MAD HATTER: Thank you!

KING: Off with his head!

MAD HATTER: WHAT?! *(runs offstage screaming madly; SOLDIERS and EXECUTIONER chase HATTER, then return)*

QUEEN: Excuse me! That's MY line!

KING: Yes, dear!

WHITE RABBIT: SECOND WITNESS!!

(COOK enters with pepper, ALL sneeze)

KING: Cook, what are the tarts made of?

COOK: Pepper, mostly.

DORMOUSE: And molasses!

QUEEN: Who asked you!? Behead that Dormouse!

DORMOUSE: NO!!! *(runs offstage screaming madly; SOLDIERS and EXECUTIONER chase DORMOUSE, then return; COOK exits unnoticed)*

KING: Where's the cook? ACHOO!!! *(to QUEEN)* Really, my dear, you must cross-examine the next witness. My head hurts!

QUEEN: Okay.

WHITE RABBIT: THIRD WITNESS!! Alice!

QUEEN: What do you know of this?

ALICE: Nothing, whatever!

QUEEN: Then, I call for a verdict!

WHITE RABBIT: Wait! Here's a note the Knave wrote.

KNAVE: That's not mine! You've no proof.

QUEEN: I want a verdict!

ALICE: But, we don't know what the note says!

WHITE RABBIT: *(reads)* They told me you had been to her, And mentioned me to him: She gave me a good character, But said I could not swim...

KING: This is the most important evidence yet!

ALICE: If it made any sense.

KING: Don't care. I want a verdict!

QUEEN: NO, NO!! Sentence first—verdict afterwards.

ALICE: That's nonsense! You just said you wanted a verdict!

QUEEN: Hold your tongue!

ALICE: NO!!!

QUEEN: OFF WITH HER HEAD!!!

ALICE: Off with my WHAT!?!? *(turns to face them)* Wait! I'm not afraid of you. You're nothing but a pack of cards!

ALL: GET HER!!!

ALICE: Ahhh!!! I just wish I was little again!!!

(ALICE exits running; ALL exit chasing her)

ACT 3 SCENE 3

(ALICE and SISTER enter; ALICE sleeps)

ALICE: *(talking in sleep)* I'm not afraid... nothing but... cards!

SISTER: Alice, wake up!

ALICE: *(wakes)* I've had such a curious dream! I followed a white rabbit down a hole and ended up in the strangest land where I kept changing size. I also met a grinning cat and a wicked queen.

SISTER: It was a curious dream! Sounds like a wonderland.

ALICE: You're right! It was a wonderland! I'm going to get some tea and a pepper tart. Would you like one?

SISTER: A pepper tart? No thanks. *(ALICE exits)* I hope when Alice is a grown woman, she'll keep her sense of wonder and imagination. Maybe, if I think about Wonderland when I fall asleep, I can visit it in my dreams. *(falls asleep)*

WHITE RABBIT: *(runs across stage)* I'm late! I'm late!

SISTER: *(wakes)* How curious!

(SISTER chases WHITE RABBIT offstage)

THE END

Special Thanks

Angela M. Herrick would like to thank Brendan, Elijah, and of course Jay. Special thanks to Orcutt Community Theater actors Dixie Arthur, Clare Terrill, Candace Colombus, Dan Bullard, Nitana de Hato Rey, Nakia Jones, Karen Silva, Brian Kasicki, Todd Buranen, Tori Buranen, Keilana Buranen, Wiley Charles, Nancy Kunishige, and Kathy Yingst for their mad readthrough skills and helpful critique.

More special thanks to Khara C. Barnhart, Isidro Rodriguez, and Dave Coonan! As always, your feedback helps these kids achieve a much richer experience with classic stories!

And a big thanks goes out to Ron Leishman for creating many of the wonderful characters for our cover!

-Brendan

Sneak Peeks at other Playing With Plays books:

Jungle Book for Kids .... Pg 85

Tempest for Kids .... Pg 87

Christmas Carol for Kids .... Pg 89

Treasure Island for Kids .... Pg 91

King Lear for Kids .... Pg 93

Beowulf for Kids .... Pg 96

Frankenstein for Kids .... Pg 98

As You Like It for Kids .... Pg 100

Sneak peek of
The Jungle Book for Kids

PARENT WOLF: Oh hi, Bagheera. What's happening in the life of a panther?

BAGHEERA: I wanted to warn you. Shere Khan's in town again.

PARENT WOLF: The tiger? What's he doing in this part of the jungle?

BAGHEERA: What tigers do. You know, hunt, eat, hunt again, eat... hunt...eat... *(trailing off)*

PARENT WOLF: *(play-acting like a tiger)* Oh look at me, I'm a mean ol' tiger, roar!!! *(there is a LOUD ROAR and GROWL from offstage, PARENT WOLF is a bit shocked)*

BAGHEERA: Listen! That's him now!

(enter MOWGLI, running off-balance, and falling down)

PARENT WOLF: Whoa! A man's cub! Look! *(ALL turn to look at MOWGLI)* How little and so... smelly, but cute! *(starts petting his hair)*

(BAGHEERA sneaks over to MOWGLI and whispers something in his ear. MOWGLI sighs and gets down on his knees to appear smaller; he remains on his knees throughout the rest of the scene and ACT1 SCENE 2)

MOWGLI: *(very sarcastically)* Gaa gaa. Goo goo.

(SHERE KHAN enters. PARENT WOLF hides MOWGLI behind her back)

SHERE KHAN: A man's cub went this way. Its parents have run off. Give it to me. I'll uh... take care of him... *(as he rubs his belly)* you can TOTALLY trust me! *(gives* *the audience a big evil smile)*

PARENT WOLF: You are NOT the boss of us.

SHERE KHAN: Excuse me?! Do you know who I am? It is I, Shere Khan, who speaks! I'm kind of a big deal. And scary! GRRRRR.

PARENT WOLF: The man's cub is mine; he shall not be killed! So beat it; you don't scare us.

SHERE KHAN: Fine. But I'll get him some day, make no mistake! Muahahahahaha! ROAR! *(SHERE KHAN exits)*

PARENT WOLF: *(to MOWGLI)* Mowgli the Frog I will call thee. Lie still, little frog.

MOWGLI: *(to PARENT WOLF)* Frog?

PARENT WOLF: *(to MOWGLI and audience)* Yeah, I guess Rudyard Kipling liked frogs! But now we have to see what the wolf leader says.

(enter AKELA, BAGHEERA, and BALOO)

AKELA: Okay, wolves, let's get this meeting started! Howl!

WOLVES: Howl!!! *(ALL WOLVES howl)*

PARENT WOLF: Akela, our great leader, I'd like to present the newest member of our pack, Mowgli the Frog!

AKELA: Hmmm, Frog, huh? If you say so.

(enter SHERE KHAN)

SHERE KHAN: ROAR! The cub is mine! Give him to me!

AKELA: Who speaks for this cub?

BALOO: *(speaking in a big, deep bear voice!)* I, Baloo the Bear, I speak for the man's cub. I myself will teach him the ways of the jungle.

Sneak peek of
The Tempest for Kids

PROSPERO: Hast thou, spirit, performed to point the tempest that I bade thee?

ARIEL: What? Was that English?

PROSPERO: *(Frustrated)* Did you make the storm hit the ship?

ARIEL: Why didn't you say that in the first place? Oh yeah! I rocked that ship! They didn't know what hit them.

PROSPERO: Why, that's my spirit! But are they, Ariel, safe?

ARIEL: Not a hair perished.

PROSPERO: Woo-hoo! All right. We've got more work to do.

ARIEL: Wait a minute. You're still going to free me, right, Master?

PROSPERO: Oh, I see. Is it sooooo terrible working for me? Huh? Remember when I saved you from that witch? Do you? Remember when that blue-eyed hag locked you up and left you for dead? Who saved you? Me, that's who!

ARIEL: I thank thee, master.

PROSPERO: I will free you in two days, okay? Sheesh. Patience is a virtue, or haven't you heard. Right. Where was I? Oh yeah... I need you to disguise yourself like a sea nymph and then... *(PROSPERO whispers something in ARIEL'S ear)* Got it?

ARIEL: Got it. *(ARIEL exits)*

PROSPERO: *(to MIRANDA)* Awake, dear heart, awake!

(MIRANDA yawns loudly)

PROSPERO: Shake it off. Come on. We'll visit Caliban, my slave.

MIRANDA: The witch's son? You mean the MONSTER! He's creepy and stinky!!!

PROSPERO: Mysterious and sneaky,

MIRANDA: Altogether freaky,

MIRANDA & PROSPERO: He's Caliban the slave!!! *(snap, snap!)*

PROSPERO: *(Calls offstage)* What, ho! Slave! Caliban!

(enter CALIBAN)

CALIBAN: Oh, look it's the island stealers! This is my home! My mother, the witch, left it to me and now you treat me like dirt.

MIRANDA: Oh boo-hoo! I used to feel sorry for you, I even taught you our language, but you tried to hurt me so now we have to lock you in that cave.

CALIBAN: I wish I had never learned your language!

PROSPERO: Go get us wood! If you don't, I'll rack thee with old cramps, and fill all thy bones with aches!

CALIBAN: *(to AUDIENCE)* He's so mean to me! But I have to do what he says. ANNOYING! *(exit CALIBAN)*

(enter FERDINAND led by "invisible" ARIEL)

ARIEL: *(Singing)* Who let the dogs out?! Woof, woof, woof!! *(Spookily)* The watchdogs bark; bow-wow, bow-wow!

FERDINAND: *(Dancing across stage)* Where should this music be? Where is it taking me! What's going on?

Sneak peek of
Christmas Carol for Kids

(enter GHOST PRESENT wearing a robe and holding a turkey leg and a goblet)

GHOST PRESENT: Wake up, Scrooge! I am the Ghost of Christmas Present. Look upon me!

SCROOGE: I'm looking. Not that impressed. But let's get on with it.

GHOST PRESENT: Touch my robe! *(SCROOGE touches GHOST PRESENT's robe. Pause. They look at each other)* Er...it must be broken. Guess we walk. Come on. *(they begin walking downstage)*

SCROOGE: Where are we going?

GHOST PRESENT: Your employee, Bob Cratchit's house. Oh look, here we are.

(enter BOB, MRS. CRATCHIT, MARTHA CRATCHIT, and TINY TIM, who has a crutch in one hand; they are all holding bowls)

BOB: *(to audience)* Hi, we're the Cratchit family. We are a REALLY happy family!

MRS. CRATCHIT: *(to audience)* Yes, but we're REALLY poor, too. Thanks to HIS boss! *(pointing at BOB)*

MARTHA: *(to audience)* Yeah, as you can see our bowls are empty. *(shows empty bowl)* We practically survive off air.

TINY TIM: *(to audience)* But we're happy!

MRS. CRATCHIT: *(to audience; overly sappy)* Because we have each other.

TINY TIM: And love!

SCROOGE: *(to GHOST PRESENT)* Seriously, are they for real?

GHOST PRESENT: Yep! Adorable, isn't it?

BOB: A merry Christmas to us all.

TINY TIM: God bless us every one!

SCROOGE: Spirit, tell me if Tiny Tim will live.

GHOST PRESENT: *(puts hands to head as if looking into the future)* Ooooo, not so good...I see a vacant seat in the poor chimney corner, and a crutch without an owner. If SOMEBODY doesn't change SOMETHING, the child will die.

SCROOGE: No, no! Say he will be spared.

GHOST PRESENT: Nope, can't do that, sorry. Unless SOMEONE decides to change... hint, hint.

BOB: A Christmas toast to my boss, Mr. Scrooge! The founder of the feast!

MRS. CRATCHIT: *(angrily)* Oh sure, Mr. Scrooge! If he were here I'd give him a piece of my mind to feast upon. What an odious, stingy, hard, unfeeling man!

BOB: Dear, it's Christmas day. He's not THAT bad. *(Pause)* He's just... THAT sad. *(BOB holds up his bowl)* Come on, kids, to Scrooge! He probably needs it more than us!

MARTHA & TINY TIM: *(holding up their bowls)* To Scrooge!

MRS. CRATCHIT: *(muttering)* Thanks for nothing.

BOB: That's not nice.

Sneak peek of
TREASURE ISLAND
for Kids

(enter JIM, TRELAWNEY, and DOCTOR; enter CAPTAIN SMOLLETT from the other side of the stage)

TRELAWNEY: Hello Captain. Are we all shipshape and seaworthy?

CAPTAIN: Trelawney, I don't know what you're thinking, but I don't like this cruise; and I don't like the men.

TRELAWNEY: *(very angry)* Perhaps you don't like the ship?

CAPTAIN: Nope, I said it short and sweet.

DOCTOR: What? Why?

CAPTAIN: Because I heard we are going on a treasure hunt and the coordinates of the island are: *(whispers to DOCTOR)*

DOCTOR: Wow! That's exactly right!

CAPTAIN: There's been too much blabbing already.

DOCTOR: Right! But, I doubt ANYTHING will go wrong!

CAPTAIN: Fine. Let's sail!

(ALL exit)

ACT 2 SCENE 3

(enter JIM, SILVER, and various other pirates)

SILVER: Ay, ay, mates. You know the song: Fifteen men on the dead man's chest.

ALL PIRATES: Yo-ho-ho and a bottle of rum!

(PIRATES slowly exit)

JIM: *(to the audience)* So, the Hispaniola had begun her voyage to the Isle of Treasure. As for Long John, well, he still is the nicest cook…

SILVER: Do you want a sandwich?

JIM: That would be great, thanks Long John! *(SILVER exits; JIM addresses audience)* As you can see, Long John is a swell guy! Until…

(JIM hides in the corner)

ACT 2 SCENE 4

(enter SILVER and OTHER PIRATES)

JIM: *(to audience)* I overheard Long John talking to the rest of the pirates.

SILVER: Listen here you, Scallywags! I was with Captain Flint when he hid this treasure. And those cowards have the map. Follow my directions, and no killing, yet. Clear?

DICK: Clear.

SILVER: But, when we do kill them, I claim Trelawney. And remember, dead men don't bite.

GEORGE: Ay, ay, Long John!

(ALL exit but JIM)

JIM: *(to audience)* Oh no! Long John Silver IS the one-legged man that Billy Bones warned me about! I have to tell the others!

(JIM runs offstage)

Sneak peek of
KING LEAR
for Kids

ACT 1 SCENE 1

KING LEAR's palace

(enter FOOL entertaining the audience with jokes, dancing, juggling, Hula Hooping... whatever the actor's skill may be; enter KENT)

KENT: Hey, Fool!

FOOL: What did you call me?!

KENT: I called you Fool.

FOOL: That's my name, don't wear it out! *(to audience)* Seriously, that's my name in the play!

(enter LEAR, CORNWALL, ALBANY, GONERIL, REGAN, and CORDELIA)

LEAR: The lords of France and Burgundy are outside. They both want to marry you, Cordelia.

ALL: Ooooooo!

LEAR: *(to audience)* Between you and me she IS my favorite child! *(to the girls)* Daughters, I need to talk to you about something. It's a really big deal.

GONERIL & REGAN: Did you buy us presents?

LEAR: This is even better than presents!

GONERIL & REGAN: Goody, goody!!!

CORDELIA: Father, your love is enough for me.

LEAR: Give me the map there, Kent. Girls, I'm tired. I've made a decision: Know that we - and by 'we' I mean 'me' - have divided in three our kingdom...

KENT: Whoa! Sir, dividing the kingdom may cause chaos! People could die!

FOOL: Well, this IS a tragedy...

LEAR: You worry too much, Kent. I'm giving it to my daughters so their husbands can be rich and powerful... like me!

CORNWALL & ALBANY: Sweet!

GONERIL & REGAN: Wait... what?

CORDELIA: This is olden times. That means that everything we own belongs to our husbands.

GONERIL & REGAN: Olden times stink!

CORDELIA: Truth.

LEAR: So, my daughters, tell your daddy how much you love him. Goneril, our eldest-born, speak first.

GONERIL: Sir, I love you more than words can say! More than outer space, puppies and cotton candy! I love you more than any child has ever loved a father in the history of the entire world, dearest Pops!

CORDELIA: *(to audience)* Holy moly! Surely, he won't be fooled by that. *(to self)* Love, and be silent.

LEAR: Thanks, sweetie! I'm giving you this big chunk of the kingdom here. What says our second daughter, Our dearest Regan, wife to Cornwall? Speak.

REGAN: What she said, Daddy... times a thousand!

CORDELIA: *(to audience)* What?! I love my father more than either of them. But I can't express it in words. My love's more richer than my tongue.

LEAR: Wow, Regan! You get this big hunk of the kingdom. Cordelia, what can you tell me to get this giant piece of kingdom as your own? Speak.

CORDELIA: Nothing, my lord.

LEAR: Nothing?!?

CORDELIA: Nothing.

LEAR: Come on, now. Nothing will come of nothing.

CORDELIA: I love you as a daughter loves her father.

LEAR: Try a little, harder, sweetie!

CORDELIA: Why are my sisters married if they give you all their love?

LEAR: How did you get so mean?

CORDELIA: Father, I will not insult you by telling you my love is like… as big as a whale.

LEAR: *(getting mad)* Fine. I'll split your share between your sisters.

REGAN, GONERIL, & CORNWALL: Yessss!

KENT: Whoa! Let's all just calm down a minute!

LEAR: Peace, Kent! You don't want to mess with me right now. I told you she was my favorite…

GONERIL & REGAN: What!?

LEAR: …and she can't even tell me she loves me more than a whale? Nope. Now I'm mad.

KENT: Royal Lear, really…

LEAR: Kent, I'm pretty emotional right now! You better not try to talk me out of this…

KENT: Sir, you're acting … insane.

Sneak peek of
BEOWULF for Kids
HROTHGAR and BEOWULF

(enter HROTHGAR and DANES)

HROTHGAR: *(wailing)* What have I done?! I have created a great hall and have put my people in danger! Hopefully, this monster will not come back again!

(exit HROTHGAR; enter GRENDEL)

GRENDEL: *(whistling; addresses audience)* Off to eat some more people! *(knocks at door, someone answers)* Rawwrr!!! I am the monster of evil, greedy and cruel, by the name of Grendel! Prepare to be eaten... again!

(GRENDEL eats some more people, wipes his mouth with a napkin, and runs off stage; enter HROTHGAR)

HROTHGAR: Nooooooo! The monster has come back and will probably keep coming back for 12 years before someone comes to help us!

(HROTHGAR and his DANES wail loudly; DANE 2 crosses the stage with a sign that says "12 Years Later"; enter BEOWULF and GEAT SOLDIERS)

BEOWULF: I, the great and mighty Beowulf, warrior and champion of the Geats, servant to King Hygelac, have heard of your sorrows and have come to help!

(ALL stop crying)

HROTHGAR: How did you hear of our sorrows?

BEOWULF: *(leaning close to HROTHGAR, whispers)* Dude, you have been crying super loud for like 12 years, and I'm right offstage over there.

HROTHGAR: *(embarrassed, wipes face)* Oh right. *(cough)* Yes. Thank you for coming to our aid!

BEOWULF: I, the great Beowulf, alone now with Grendel I shall manage the matter, with the monster of evil.

HROTHGAR: Whew, that's a relief! I have been trying to figure out how to defeat Grendel for years and have failed. He's stopped by 4,380 times to feast on us!

BEOWULF: I never fail! I have defeated many a monster in my day! Including a sea monster... which is extra cool.

UNFERTH: Boooooo. That sea monster wasn't even that big!

BEOWULF: Who are you? And YES IT WAS!

UNFERTH: I am Unferth, great warrior for Hrothgar.

BEOWULF: *(to audience)* Obviously not THAT great. *(to UNFERTH)* You are just jealous of my greatness!

UNFERTH: Am not!

BEOWULF: Are too! And I heard you killed your brothers!

UNFERTH: Wow, that's a low blow... but... uhhhhh.... okay fine. I'll hang out right over here...

HROTHGAR: ANYWAY, back to me and MY problems.

BEOWULF: Right. Only with hand-grip the foe I must grapple, fight for my life then. If he win in the struggle, to eat in the war-hall earls of the geat-folk, boldly to swallow them.

GEAT SOLDIER 1: Wait... what was that?

BEOWULF: Sorry, quoting old text there.... I am going to fight Grendel with my bare hands. If I win, he dies. If I lose, he gets to eat all of us, including you!

Sneak peek of
FRANKENSTEIN for Kids
ACT 1 SCENE 1

(enter WALDMAN and VICTOR)

WALDMAN: Victor! Come in! You look so tired.

VICTOR: I'm fine, Professor Waldman! I've been working on an experiment. There's so much to be done.

WALDMAN: You remind me of myself as a young student! So few of us are willing to give our right arms for science!

VICTOR: You have no idea! *(to audience)* I will solve the mysteries of creation! *(laughs madly)*

WALDMAN: Pardon me?

VICTOR: I said...ahhh... I need a vacation! Gotta go back to work. Excuse me! *(VICTOR exits)*

WALDMAN: Strange kid.

(WALDMAN exits; VICTOR pops back on stage and addresses audience)

VICTOR: He'd think I'm mad if I told him! I've figured out how to make dead things live again! *(laughs madly, exits and returns with arms and legs)* I've been through dozens of graves and hospitals. Finally, I have everything I need!

(exits, laughing madly)

ACT 1 SCENE 2

(MONSTER is laying under a sheet; VICTOR enters)

VICTOR: *(to audience)* I see by your eagerness that you expect to see how it's done. Ha! If I showed you, you'd be...SHOCKED! Time to become the world's first bodybuilder! *(VICTOR laughs madly as he raises the sheet to hide himself and MONSTER)* To bolt or not to bolt, THAT is the question! *(there's a clap of thunder, then VICTOR yanks away sheet)*

MONSTER: *(sits up in monster voice)* GRR!!! GRR!!!

VICTOR: It's alive! It's alive!! IT'S ALIVE!!!

MONSTER: You never said that in the book!

VICTOR: I know but, it's more fun to say...IT'S ALIVE!

MONSTER: *(MONSTER takes one step towards VICTOR)* GRR!!!

VICTOR: OK!!! AAGH!!! Monster! *(screams and runs to other side of stage)*

MONSTER: Now THAT'S what you said in the book! ARGHHH!!!

(VICTOR runs away screaming, MONSTER takes the sheet and wears it like a cloak, exits)

Sneak peek of
AS YOU LIKE IT
for Kids
ACT 1 SCENE 2
DUKE FREDRICK'S PALACE

(enter CELIA and ROSALIND)

CELIA: I pray thee, Rosalind, sweet my coz, be merry.

ROSALIND: If you can teach me how to forget a banished father, then I'll be merry.

CELIA: Tell ya what, when my father dies, I'll give you the kingdom back. Therefore, my dear Rose, be merry!

ROSALIND: Cool! I'm bored. I know! What think you of falling in love?

CELIA: Sounds like fun! *(enter TOUCHSTONE)* Well, hello clown, how are you today?

TOUCHSTONE: Joke: What was the nickname for the knight who ruled the fort? Fortnight!

ROSALIND: Ha ha! *(pauses)* I don't get it.

TOUCHSTONE: You know, fort-knight... aghh, nevermind. Here come the Duke and the wrestlers.

(enter DUKE FREDRICK, CHARLES, ORLANDO, and DOTING LORD saying random wonderful things about the duke)

DUKE F.: How now, daughter and niece, here to see the wrestling?

CELIA: Yep!

ROSALIND: *(to ORLANDO)* Hey, that guy's pretty strong. Are you sure you want to get your butt kicked?

ORLANDO: *(warming up and not noticing ROSALIND)* Me? Hah! I will beat him with the strength of my youth! *(poses)*

CELIA: You know, this is the perfect time to panic and run.

ORLANDO: Bah! My brother detests me and I have little money, so I have nothing left to lose. Let's rumble!

DUKE F: *(addresses audience)* Ladies and gentlemen! In this corner, Charles the Magnificent! *(EVERYONE cheers)* and in this corner... *(to ORLANDO)* Uh... what's your name, kid?

ORLANDO: *(thinks)*... Captain O!

DUKE F: Captain O? K, he's going to get smashed!!! *(ROSALIND and CELIA cheer)*

CHARLES: Charles, SMASH!!!

ROSALIND: Now Hercules be thy speed, young man!

(they wrestle and ORLANDO wins)

DUKE F: What is thy name, young man?

ORLANDO: Orlando, my liege.

DUKE F: As in Sir Roland's son? My enemy? Humph!!! Now I'm mad! Let's leave.

(DUKE F and DOTING LORD exit)

ORLANDO: I am proud to be Sir Roland's son.

ROSALIND: My father loved Sir Roland.

ORLANDO: *(stunned by ROSALIND'S beauty)* Ahhh... wow... ohhh...

CELIA: *(pats ORLANDO on the back)* Well said, Captain O. Shall we go, coz?

ROSALIND: Hey, you're kinda cute.

ORLANDO: Ahhh...ohhh...

ROSALIND: Fare you well.

(CELIA and ROSALIND exit)

ORLANDO: *(to audience)* What passion hangs these weights upon my tongue? *(mocking himself)* Ahhhh... ohhhh... I'm such a fool! But, I gotta go! From tyrant duke unto a tyrant brother, how fun! But, heavenly Rosalind!

(ALL exit)

ABOUT THE AUTHORS

ANGELA M. HERRICK is a drama teacher, actor, writer, and director and has a passion for storytelling. A teacher at heart, she believes in retelling these classic stories in a way that makes them fun and accessible for the next generation. Angela lives on the Central Coast of California and loves hanging out with her husband, five children, Savannah the dog, and cats Gatsby and Mayhem.

BRENDAN P. KELSO came to writing modified Shakespeare scripts when he was taking time off from work to be at home with his newly born son. "It just grew from there". Within months, he was being asked to offer classes in various locations and acting organizations along the Central Coast of California. Originally employed as an engineer, Brendan never thought about writing. However, his unique personality, humor, and love for engaging the kids with The Bard has led him to leave the engineering world and pursue writing as a new adventure in life! He has always believed, "the best way to learn is to have fun!" Brendan makes his home on the Central Coast of California and loves to spend time with his wife and kids.

CAST AUTOGRAPHS

Made in the USA
Monee, IL
07 June 2022